Dedication

I would like to dedicate this book first to my wife of Forty-One and a Half years, Beverly. She has been with me from the start. We married six months before I began my first appointment in Arkport. She is a woman of deep faith, inexhaustible patience and a good sense of humor. Bev has always been extolled by the congregations I have served. In fact, sometimes (many times?) she is missed more than I am. The reader will find the fragrance of her presence in many of these "Reflections."

Then I must mention our beautiful children. I have included them in a few of these humorous vignettes. They have been our special gifts in our journey together. We married late, although our ages at the time - "28" and "30"- are common in today's matrimonial culture. Jed came along after seven years, Jeanna sixteen months later and finally Joy, the day before Bev turned 42! Somehow, they appear to have attained my wackiness.

Finally, I am thankful for the wonderful bouquet of personalities I was privileged to serve as pastor for thirty-three years plus. I have been blessed beyond my wildest imagination and am thankful to the Lord.

Jeff

Introduction

These "Reflections" waited a long time to be served as they simmered in my comedic slow cooker. I have often entertained myself and others as I recalled the unique people and events at their center. My sense of humor was readily provoked by the flow of life as a pastor.

I am sure that pastoral ministry will not go well if one is not able to see the humor in circumstances and situations that all too often appear to support the observation that truth is sometimes stranger than fiction. It is obvious that I have a wacky streak (which I attribute to my mom).

In fact, a sense of humor is important to any endeavor in life. That being true, no one, in reading these "Reflections" should think that I just laughed my way through thirty-three years of pastoral ministry. I could easily write a book about the sad and tragic things that occurred. These involved precious persons being deeply wounded by an unexpected death, marital brokenness, and other kinds of loss. I was "on call" 24/7 and needed to respond when trouble happened.

I have been especially blessed to have a wife of 41 years who has usually laughed with me when I have found someone or something humorous. There have been times when she has had to just roll with it when I burst into laughter in the middle of the night thinking about the craziness of life. Our children inherited the ability to find the humor in life and it has helped them in their vocations.

You will see that this book begins with two reflections which I have intentionally not attached to a specific place. It is important to protect the identity of the persons involved. The rest are placed within their respective locations, excepting two reflections following retirement (After all, once a pastor always a pastor!)

It is my hope that these sixty "Humorous Reflections" will resonate with some and refresh many. May you laugh and be thankful to our Gracious God as you are reminded of the imperfections that permeate us all.

Acknowledgement

I want to thank my 92-year-old Uncle, Jack Crawford, and my 90-year-old Aunt, Maurine Crawford, for doing a "cold read" of this book and suggesting several grammatical corrections.

For the most part they were incorporated into these humorous reflections.

"Humorous Reflections"

TABLE OF CONTENTS

"Newsletter Blooper"   13

"Waking Snoozie"   14

Arkport

1976 – 1987

"Minnie and Lou – Episode One"   18

"Minnie and Lou – Episode Two"   21

"Minnie and Lou – Episode Three"   23

"Minnie and Lou – Episode Four"   25

"Dorcas"   27

"Silent Night"   29

"Goin to Kansas City"   31

"Bell Rung"   33

"Damn It!"   35

"Pot N Pans Band"   37

"Pastor Paul – Episode One"   39

"Pastor Paul – Episode Two and Three"   42

"Pastor Paul – Episode Four"   45

"Pastor's Delight"   47

"Y Ball"   51

"Foiled!"   53

"Tom's Magic"   56

"U Turn" 59

"The Ax Handle Award" 61

"Hot Wheels" 64

Barker: Faith

1987 – 1991

"Vanishing Shoes" 68

"Chigar Shmokin Boosher" 70

"Sarah" 72

"Christmas Fireworks" 74

"Joy" 76

"Pushing Buttons" 78

Olean District

1991 – 1995

"String Music" 82

"Earl's Garage" 85

"Ticked Off" 87

"Bag Lady" 90

"Mimic" 93

"Cat Tales" 96

"Beer Party" 100

"Stripper" 103

Penfield

1995 – 2004

"Hyena"	107
"The Incredible Enlarging Machine"	110
"Why, it's the Pastor"	113
"Santa Clod"	116
"Max's Place"	119
"Septic Dining"	122
"We saw that Dad!"	125
"Lil Wayne"	128
"Squirminator"	131
"Rone"	134
"Let'r Blow"	137
"Kamikazi Sushi Bar"	140
"Mack's Wild Kingdom"	143
"Broken Every Law of Moving!"	148

Canandaigua

2004 – 2009

"Bat Tongs"   152

"Flying Air Conditioner"   156

"Communion Stumble"   159

"I'm going to Put It Down"   162

"Cop Stop"   165

"Cemetery Unzipped"   168

"Terminator and Jesus"   171

"Celebration!"   175

Post Retirement

2009 – Present

"Squeeky"   180

"Brother Greg"   183

"Newsletter Blooper"

Newsletter and Bulletin Bloopers are widely known. They have provided many a laugh. Virtually every Administrative Assistant, Office Manager or Secretary has been responsible for a blooper or two. The one that I still find the most hilarious of all I have seen is the one described below.

I had an Administrative Assistant in one of my churches who handed me her first newsletter to proof. It was fine until the article someone had submitted about opportunities for ministry. One suggestion in the article was "visiting shut-ins in the nursing home." Somehow "i" got substituted for "u" in "shut." Well, I burst out laughing and wrote "this would really stink" in the margin. I gave it back to the Assistant but heard nothing. Later that day I asked her if she had caught my reference to the blooper. With a very red face she exclaimed, "Yes! I am so glad you saw that!"

"Waking Snoozie!"

So, the challenge of all preachers is keeping people awake. Even great preachers have people fall asleep, usually because they have jobs that demand late nights, they have a sleep disorder, or they have grown used to the voice and cadence of the "great preacher." It was no different when I ascended the Pulpit.

There were instances where folks just couldn't keep their eyes open during my scintillating sermons! And since I always maintained good eye contact with my congregations, I knew who these persons were.

Well, more than once I did things to startle a sleeper into waking up!! The time I chuckle about the most is when a perpetrator seemed to decide once again it was nap time when I began one of my Biblical expositions. I kept glancing at "Snoozie" and finally, at an appropriate time, I went down into the mike on the pulpit and virtually shouted something!! At that moment, my brother in Christ, jumped awake like he had been hit with a bolt of lightning!! He DID crack a smile and all of this began a chain reaction!! The people around him were visibly bouncing in their pews as they tried to contain their laughter!!

It didn't ultimately solve the "problem."

ARKPORT

1976 - 1987

"MINNIE AND LOU – EPISODE ONE"

I met Minnie and Lou when they sought me out for counseling. They were having friction in their relationship and wanted to know what direction I would suggest. They were 50-ish and each had been married twice. After listening to what was going on and since they were not married but living together, I suggested that they either go their separate ways or get married. To my utter amazement they decided to get hitched and asked me to do the honor.

So, we set the wedding for noon on a Saturday at the Arkport UMC (where I was serving my first appointment out of seminary). And since they had gotten to know Bev a little they asked her to be their organist. Bev is a great pianist but an organist? Not so much. She practiced a couple of numbers and began playing at about 11:45. The wedding was delayed because a bus load of their coworkers, bus drivers for the City of Rochester, had not shown up yet. Finally, at 12:30, this City Bus came to a screeching halt next to the church building and a raucous bunch of folks came pouring into the sanctuary.

The service began and almost immediately one of the groomsmen collapsed, drooping across the altar rail. I had just begun a solemn prayer and when I heard the thud and Minnie scream "Oh my God, Jimmy's fainted!" (Jimmy was Minnie's 27-year-old son and he had spent the night before drinking) I did not want to open my eyes. Seminary had not prepared me for something like this! Well, fortunately a lay leader, who along with many people were there from the congregation supporting Minnie and Lou, had the calm disposition to help get Jimmy up and outside for some fresh air.

We got through the ceremony without further incident and bus driver Minnie, who had managed to squeeze into her original wedding gown, veil and all, got on that City Bus and drove it, loaded with her new husband, Louis, and all those fellow bus drivers, up to the Dansville Legion, fifteen miles north.

I understand that a couple of people coming down Rt. 36 almost drove off the road when they saw that spectacle - a veiled bride driving a bus coming at them from the opposite direction!!

"MINNIE AND LOU – EPISODE TWO"

Minnie and Lou were, simply put, salt-of-the-earth people, and we considered them special friends. During the wedding ceremony (described in the episode one), they had a reel to reel tape recorder running. This recorder had been placed on a little table between them and me.

On occasion, they would invite Bev and I and our little ones, Jed and Jeanna, up to their place for a Sunday picnic after church. Their humble abode was a kind of double wide mobile home. I say, "kind of a double wide" because somehow two single mobile homes had been put together with a roof over both! It was comfortable and unique.

Well, they had nailed a speaker to the outside of one end that reminded me of something from the "Mash" series. And during our picnic lunch we were treated to the blaring of the tape recording of the wedding ceremony.

We always waited with anticipation to hear once again Minnie exclaim, "OH MY GOD, JIMMY'S FAINTED!"

"MINNIE AND LOU – EPISODE THREE"

Minnie and Lou made a unique couple. Occasionally I would stop by their place just to check in. One time I discovered that they had added to their family - an Albino Skunk! I honestly don't remember its name but they assured me that it had had its scent gland removed! THAT was a relief but it kept lurking behind the couch I was sitting on and I was just waiting for that snorting little carnivore to bite my ankle.

I finally asked Minnie to please put the skunk somewhere else. So, she took a big piece of plywood and angled it across the entrance to the kitchen. I spent the rest of my visit listening to this critter scratch, snort and cry behind the barrier.

Some months later during a visit I noticed the absence of skunk sounds and asked, "so where is your pet skunk?" Minnie said, "Let me show you!" She took me over to a chest freezer in the dining area and popped up the lid. There was what's-its-name, frozen stiff inside a plastic bag! There had been a death in the family since my last visit!!

The intention was to take the little stiff to a taxidermist, so that Minnie and Lou would have fond memories in more than just photos. The conclusion of this episode was that on a later visit the skunk was baaaaaack..., and it was stuffed and perched on a shelf in some sort of typical pet skunk posture, and able to be appreciated in perpetuity!

"MINNIE AND LOU – EPISODE FOUR"

There are other side-splitting episodes in my pastoral and friendship journey with Minnie and Lou. At least two of these will remain unwritten because of the need for confidentiality. Some have wondered what happened to this special and beloved couple.

Unfortunately, their marriage didn't last and they went their separate ways, at least for a while. After we left Arkport, Lou was diagnosed with terminal cancer. He eventually went to live with a daughter in the Rochester area. One day when I was serving the Barker Faith congregation, Minnie called and asked if Bev and I could come and visit Lou. She was there helping to take care of him and it was as though they never divorced. We had a wonderful time of reminiscing and prayer that included some laughter as you can imagine.

After Lou died, Minnie wanted to give money in his memory to our Barker church. I was somewhat stumped as to what to say until I remembered that we were in the process of buying new hymnals. Then I suggested that she buy 10 of these and we would place memorial plates in each one. The funny thing about this is that there are nine of these (we took one when we left) still in use and if anyone looks at who they are dedicated to, they will see: "Presented to the glory of God in memory of Louis by Minnie." And they could very well wonder "who are, or were, these people?!"

Well, now anyone who read about Minnie and Lou through these reflections knows a little about this salt-of-the earth lovable couple. (Minnie died several years ago and I believe they had a wonderful reunion in heaven.)

"DORCAS"

Dorcas, was more than a memorable personality in the life of Arkport UMC. She could not come to church because of physical infirmities so I visited on a regular basis, often taking communion to her. The first thing she said to me when I entered her home was, "visit the chicken." She had a glass chicken where she kept candy and so I HAD to have one - it was a ritual.

Dorcas had been raised in the Salvation Army and more than once she told me the story of how as a little girl she had sat on the lap of founder, William Booth, and yanked on his long white beard. She also taught me several songs, one of which was this: "I'm climbing up the golden stairs to glory, climbing with the golden crown before me. I'm climbing in the light, climbing day and night, and I'll SHOUT with all my might when I get there!"

Eventually Dorcas went to live in the Steuben County Infirmity, so I traveled there to visit her. She always had two or more boxes of Captain Crunch on top of a dresser which she munched on as often as possible.

One day when I was there and talking to her about her daily routines, she told me about how she was doing the "Wiggle Diggle." After I questioned her about this she proceeded to show me. She sat in her wheel chair and began a completely spastic flailing of her arms and body and that caught me so off guard that I immediately burst into laughter. This unique soul more than lived up to her Biblical name!!

"SILENT NIGHT"

In the same mobile home park where Dorcas lived there was a man who lived alone. During one Christmas Season, carolers from our church were urged to serenade him with Christmas songs to soothe his loneliness. *(As was our pattern, a few nights before Christmas, a number of youth and adults formed a choir with me playing my trumpet for accompaniment.)*

So, we proceeded to array ourselves just outside of his front door and sing away. Like always, I was blasting away on my horn. We got no response. It was a crisp December night with snowflakes gently falling. Only a single night light appeared to be on inside. So, we moved to our closing song which was "Silent Night."

Suddenly, in the dim light, we saw movement and we were prepared for this gentleman to open his door and express gratitude for our thoughtfulness during this special season. Instead, the door flew open with a bang and we were greeted with a barrage of yelling that went something like this: "You are singing 'Silent Night'...WELL I WANT SILENCE!"

I can tell you that from that moment until this day - about 30 years have passed - singing "Silent Night" has never been the same!!

"GOIN TO KANSAS CITY"

O ur first family car was a green 60's vintage Rambler four door sedan. I called it the "Mean Green Mochine." Bev brought this into our marriage. Well, Bev, and our good friend Terry (mentioned in the "U Turn" Reflection.), and I were on our way back from the Area Youth for Christ Annual Banquet.   The Arkport congregation significantly supported this ministry now known as Family Life Ministries.

We were on the Southern Tier Expressway listening to a World Series playoff game, involving the Kansas City Royals (I spent my early years living in the Kansas City area) when near a place called Howard the Mean Green Mochine just stopped. I am somewhat dependent on Terry's recollection for some of this but neither of us can remember the issue: battery, alternator, ran out of gas? But there we were on a crisp October night, pitch black, and stuck in the middle of a little more than nowhere. It very well might have been the "run out of gas" issue because Terry remembers Bev being less than pleased.

At any rate, Terry offered to go to his apartment in Arkport and get his car. He flagged down someone by almost jumping in front of them. A young couple, with a baby in the back seat, graciously stopped and provided Terry transportation back to his place. It took him longer to return because apparently, he couldn't remember exactly where we were. This made Bev even more upset.

The wacky part involves what I did when initially exiting the Mean Green Mochine and in the face of this unexpected and totally frustrating turn of events - this breakdown. I belted out "WE'RE GOIN TO KANSAS CITY, KANSAS CITY HERE WE COME, THEY'VE GOT SOME CRAZY LITTLE WOMEN THERE AND I'M GOING TO GET ME ONE" (I already had a little woman who was significantly less than crazy - ticked off maybe - but not crazy.)

"BELL RUNG!"

Dorothy had deep roots in the Arkport congregation. Her father had been an early pillar in the church. We have a rocking chair in our living room that belonged to him which we purchased very reasonably from Dorothy. While I was the pastor there she became overwhelmed with the mission to get our church bell ringing.

My office was located up in the bell tower just below the bell. So... every Sunday someone was selected to yank on the rope suspended inside my office and clang the community awake to the fact that our service was about to begin. I must admit I was not a complete fan of this because I tried to use the time before the service in my office to center and prepare for leading and preaching. I simply had to deal as graciously as I could with this disruption.

This all turned hilarious one Sunday when the precious sister designated for bell ringing duty reached up as high as she could, pulled down on the rope, but then forgot to let go when the rope flew up! The bell clanged and there she was, suspended off the floor with her head pushing up one of the ceiling tiles. I ran over and pulled her and the rope down and as gently as I could reminded her, "you have to let go of the rope."

"DAMN IT!"

I have the permission of our daughter, Jeanna Colleen, to share this reflection. (Jeanna is named after Colleen Weekley, a wonderful woman in the Arkport congregation.) In Arkport, we had a Fifth Sunday Fellowship. This gave folks who might have to go home after church and eat alone an opportunity to enjoy fellowship and a nice meal at a local restaurant.

One fifth Sunday my parents had come to visit from the Jamestown, NY area and on this day, we had a larger than normal group assemble. They had put several tables together so that we could be one big happy church family. Jeanna was nearing three years old at this time. For the most part, the conversation was jovial as we prepared to receive our meals. I say, "for the most part" because Bev and I were dealing with our daughter's inability to stay seated. It was the old "ants in your pants" thing that sometimes overwhelms children who must sit very long. But it was annoying and embarrassing us.

We kept speaking to her and even physically helping her to SIT DOWN. Finally, apparently Jeanna's frustration with us

trumped our frustration with her. Our sweet little daughter got out of her chair, stepped away from the table, jumped up and down and exclaimed "DAMN IT!"

There was this burst of laughter around the table and slightly red faced I said, "I have NO idea where she could have gotten that." For some reason, there was a new eruption of laughter.

"POTS 'N PANS BAND"

My Arkport reflections would not be complete without describing our "Pots and Pans" Band. I know I will continue to remember all kinds of funny stuff from every place I served as a pastor but this has to be one of the most hilarious. It wasn't long after arriving in Arkport that we were initiated into "the band." It took a group of people with a great sense of humor - adults mind you - to march around playing kazoos and beating on pots and pans. But that's exactly what we did.

We were entertainment for "appropriate" church functions as well as celebrants for special occasions. Bev remembers the Pots and Pans Band arriving at the parsonage to help boom, buzz and bang us into our second year of marriage!!

Suddenly, to this day, I find myself uncontrollably erupting into, "boom chick a chick, boom chick a chick, boom chick a chick chick...BOOM BOOM!" This provided the rhythm for songs like "When the Saints go Marching In," played on kazoos with drum beats provided by hitting pots and pans with whatever...

Our fearless and nutty band director was Ruthie, who would bring us to "order" by raising her hands and saying something like "ok, come on now." We would "tune" our kazoos and off we would go. Ruthie was a sweet woman who had quite a funny bone. She is probably directing a Heavenly Pots and Pans Band right now. "Boom chick a chick, boom chick a chick, boom chick a chick chick, BOOM BOOM!"

"PASTOR PAUL – EPISODE ONE"

I have a few more reflections from my time serving the Arkport UMC. As you might expect, being in a place for eleven years, the longest of any of my appointments, many humorous incidents and episodes continued to bubble up.

Pastor Paul, the Presbyterian, became a special friend during my years in Arkport. Paul came to his first parish in Canaseraga a year after I began serving my first appointment in Arkport. Only a few miles separated our churches, located in small villages not far from Hornell, NY. Paul did serve two churches, The United Church of Canaseraga and the Ossian Presbyterian Church. Don't ask me where Ossian is...well...it's not far from Poag's Hole where they have the renowned Poag's Hole Hill Climb every year-to this day a dirt bike competition advertised all over our area.

Paul had an incisive and somewhat devious mind. I guess that last part helped us become so close during these formatives years of pastoral ministry.

Some of our experiences reflected the fact that sometimes truth is stranger than fiction.

During those days, several churches in the small communities around where Paul and I served joined together for Lenten/Good Friday services. Paul, Pastor Dan of Burns Community Church and I were the architects of this group and we called it the Arkport-Canaseraga Fellowship of Churches. One Sunday night, Paul used a two-reel film he had rented that came with explicit instructions about which reel to play first. Well, somehow, he (of the incisive mind) played the second reel first. I thought something was funny but for some reason it didn't seem that far out of whack, until he switched reels! I never let him forget that one.

On another night, also during a Lenten Sunday evening, it was my turn to preach in the Ossian Presbyterian Church. At that time of the year the cluster flies that inhabit small churches were beginning to wake up and make their annoying presence known by doing their lazy flying and buzzing around, into and onto anything and anyone. Standing at the pulpit, I had just made one of my salient points and felt like my sermon was so good I wanted to take notes on myself, when one of those flies fell onto my open Bible. It began what I can only describe as a death spin. I HAD to do something fast so I took my hand, raised it as high as I could without folks thinking I was signaling "Hallelujah" and SMACKED that fly into oblivion.

It startled more than a few people who were in a state of rapture...or possibly asleep. I guess, looking back, it helped punctuate that point.   But afterwards I picked on Pastor Paul for sending the fly from hell to disrupt my captivating oracle.

"PASTOR PAUL – EPISODES TWO AND THREE"

So, Pastor Paul, the Presbyterian, who served the Canaseraga Larger Parish just a few miles from Arkport, became a close friend. Like all of us in some way, Paul was a brother who exhibited some contradictions.

One of these involved his determination to not eat sugar. Both he and his wife, Priscilla, felt the same way. So, when I was in their home and they served me coffee there would be this scramble to find the sugar bowl. They had one but "hid" it so not to be tempted. Paul would rifle through cupboards in order to accommodate my need for sugar for my coffee. (I have since, for many years, learned to drink coffee black.) I found this to be humorous in a ridiculous sort of way.

So absolutely NO sugar in the life of Pastor Paul until the time we were traveling together to attend a continuing education event.

Paul insisted we stop at a Donut shop, allegedly for coffee. I remember this being in the Elmira, NY area.

While in this place Paul spied cream-filled delights and to my utter amazement not only bought some but devoured several as we continued our trip! I guess sugar consumed in that way was ok.

Another incident worthy of mention occurred on this trip. Brother Bruce, an Assembly of God pastor on the edge of Hornell, was driving his Volvo. I was convinced a Volvo was just about invincible until we started smelling something burning. We ended up in a garage where we had to spend several hours waiting for a part to be replaced. As we stood around twiddling our thumbs an older guy with a weathered face and an ill temperament appeared carrying a flat tire. He repeatedly exclaimed, "Jesus Christ!" as he stared at the tire. Finally, Paul stepped over, peered into the tire and declared, "I don't see Jesus Christ in there!"

Paul had to have hernia surgery at some later point and I felt it was my privilege and duty to provide support and encouragement. After all we were not only colleagues but good friends. So right after he returned to the parsonage from this procedure I called him and said I would be over - to make him laugh. The next day I sat beside his bed doing my best to test those stitches in his abdomen. After all, what are pillows, ice and friends for?!

Mind you, I never treated a parishioner this way. Almost Never.

"PASTOR PAUL – EPISODE FOUR"

Some may wonder what happened to Pastor Paul, the Presbyterian. He left the area when he was called to be the Associate Pastor of a Presbyterian Church in Connecticut. I had the privilege of participating in his installation in that large and affluent congregation.

I know he was a busy parson with a wife, three children (all born while he and Priscilla were in Canaseraga) and a demanding schedule. But in the following years I could not get him to respond to even Christmas Letters we would send from Arkport and then Barker. I thought, what kind of good friend and colleague, who has endured all of my shenanigans, would just jettison our connection no matter how busy they are?!

So, one Christmas while I was in Barker, I decided to try one more time to get this guy to communicate! I had Bev take a picture of me laying under our Christmas tree on Christmas morning with a bow on my head, wearing my jammies. I sent it to Paul with no return address and nothing written inside the envelope, just the photo. I STILL got no response!!!

(Well, Paul has served as the pastor of the Faith Presbyterian Church in Cranston, Rhode Island, for the last 20 to 25 years. The congregation has thrived under his excellent leadership and he is about to retire. We exchange Christmas letters every other year or so and he has threatened to come and stay with us, with Priscilla, of course.)

PASTORS' DELIGHT

(I was dependent on recollections from
Rev. Paul Terry for this Reflection)

My Reflections would be incomplete without a follow-up to the four episode focus on Pastor Paul the Presbyterian. During my stay in Arkport I had an unmatched experience with colleagues and collegial fellowship. This involved the same group of pastors who served the congregations in the Arkport-Canaseraga Fellowship of Churches. Some pretty comical things happened as we lived out our bond of mutual support.

The primary cogs in this unique fellowship were Pastor Paul (Canaseraga Larger Parish and Ossian Presbyterian Church), Pastor Dan (Burns Community Church), Pastor "Rocky" (Garwoods and Swain United Methodist Churches), Pastor Elton (Canaseraga Wesleyan Church), Pastor Pete (Arkport Presbyterian Church) and yours truly. Together we formed quite a bouquet of personalities... or... quite a motley crew.

Paul and I were fresh out of seminary, Rocky and Pete were second career pastors and Elton and Dan had served churches for many years.

We were in the habit of meeting for breakfast every month or so in one another's parsonages. This gave us a regular occasion to check in with each other and enjoy food, fellowship and prayer. On one occasion, we met in the Swain parsonage. As we chatted Paul asked Rocky when he was going to change the message on his Garwood's church sign. And for the benefit of those of us who had not taken note of it, Paul added, it reads, "PENTECOST POWER!" This was in the fall, much beyond the observance of Pentecost. Rocky's response made us all laugh while nodding our approval: "Someone else asked me the same question a few days ago. I told her that I wasn't going to change the sign until the people "GET IT!" "PENTECOST POWER!", remained on the sign at least into the winter!

During each Lenten Season, the Fellowship of Churches hosted services occurring on Sunday evenings, Good Friday and Easter Sunday – a sunrise service with breakfast. (I referred to this in one of the "Pastor Paul" reflections.) We took turns preaching at these events. During our planning for one of these Lenten series, Rocky had been assigned the Good Friday responsibility. It was our habit to gather for prayer in the Pastor's Study of the church where the service was to take place. I remember our forming a prayer circle in the Arkport Presbyterian Church Study and praying something like this: "Oh, Lord, take the message Rocky has prepared and touch the hearts of those gathered – may it be a powerful reminder of Jesus' death on the cross!" Immediately following the last "Amen," Rocky exclaimed, "YOU MEAN I'M PREACHING?!" As he said this he was rifling through his pocket calendar and sure enough, there it was!! The rest of us "brothers of the cloth" marveled at the message he produced on a "Wing and a Prayer!" And you couldn't wipe the smiles off our faces!

One last wacky memory involves a particular Easter Sunrise Service outside of the Arkport Village Cemetery. The cemetery is located at the end of a unique main street that dead ends on both ends! So,

the cemetery is a "dead end" in more ways than one.
Well, a hardy throng of early birds and stout of heart
had gathered. The sun was just beginning to burn
through the fog, the tombstones were becoming more
visible reminders of death, breakfast was awaiting us
in the warmth of the Arkport United Methodist Church
Fellowship Hall (just a short walk away), and about
sixty of us were waiting for Pete to start our teeth-
chattering celebration of Jesus' resurrection. He was
nowhere to be seen, until the end, when he came
running up the street. As we concluded, I asked him to
offer the benediction, since he had missed delivering
the invocation. We got the... invocation. Apparently,
his bell had not completely rung!!

Nothing in the way of collegial fellowship ever
came close to this
unique and
sometimes
hilarious
experience.
This was truly a
Pastors' Delight.

"Y BALL"

I always tried to find some way to exercise as a pastor. First, I jogged, but then at about 35 years of age, I rediscovered the joy of basketball. Almost all YMCA's have noon time men's basketball. Everywhere I served as a pastor I joined the local Y and as often as I could, I would try to prove why I just missed being drafted by the NBA. One" Y" called this program "Elbows for Lunch."

This all began at the Hornell Y (near Arkport). The motley crew - lawyers, business types, blue- collar workers, pastors - who came in to play at lunch at this Y had less to prove than at any other Y I experienced. Wackiness permeated our play. Many had nicknames like "Hands of Stone", "Chewie" and "Chief Mugger." The moniker "Chief Mugger" belonged to the local police chief.   If he was playing defense anywhere close to you when you tried to drive to the basket you'd better have one hand on your shorts and one hand on the ball! Otherwise you might find yourself with your pants around your knees!

The local Cable TV owner was there quite often and he was mercilessly picked on. He had certain standards for programming and that meant MTV was terminated. At that time, there was a wildly popular MTV music video titled "Money for Nothing" by Dire Straits. It included the lyric "I want my MTV." These guys would surround him in the locker room and let him have it with "I WANT MY MTV!"

I want my young knees...

"FOILED!"

Two special people in the Arkport congregation were Doris and Les. Les was the manager of the Girl Scout Camp nearby. Doris was like a grandma to Jed and Jeanna. I don't remember how many times we enjoyed a Sunday-after-Service meal in their home. I especially loved Doris' spaghetti and meatballs and her stewed tomatoes served with ham. Once we got to their "Cookie House" it was relaxation time after doing all that work leading worship, preaching and teaching Senior High Sunday School, which I did for ten of my eleven years in Arkport.

Sometimes it was a bit stressful getting the little ones bundled into the car for the trip up Oak Hill Road and out to the camp. Many times, Bev and I have looked back and laughed about a couple of things that happened getting our act together, as they say.

Like the time that we were well up West Avenue and Bev shouted, "THE PIE!" She remembered putting a frozen pie wrapped in tin foil on top of the car while she buckled in one of the kids. I looked in the rear-view mirror and there it was, laying on the street, upside down. Fortunately, "The Pie" was still covered with foil although it did have a few indentations on the top from hitting the pavement at an unknown speed! As I recall it was still edible - maybe a bit crunchy....

But the second incident was funnier. We had returned home from church like always, picked up a frozen loaf of Banana Bread, like the aforementioned pie wrapped in tin foil, wrestled the kids into car seats, and had made it up West Avenue. We were just starting up Oak Hill when Bev remembered something else she wanted to take to Doris. I was in no mood for having to turn the car around and go back home. Apparently, I was making my displeasure known as I whipped the car into someone's driveway when WHAM!! That frozen foil wrapped loaf of Banana Bread had whizzed just past my face and slammed against my driver side window! I got the wake-up call I deserved!!

(That was one of only two times I remember Bev hurling something at me, other than an occasional wet dishcloth or...).

"TOM'S MAGIC"

An annual event for the Arkport UMC was its "Talent Night." A number of, would be entertainers would sign up to share their "talent." This included sweet children singing or playing an instrument and adults putting on some sort of act. It evoked the full range of emotions from worshipful to wacky.

Each year, the signature act was Tom's "Magic." Tom would ascend the platform in the front of the sanctuary and immediately the chuckles would begin. He could be described as having a drollness to his personality and a kind of dry sense of humor that could surprise you. Tom's "Magic" was a take-off of a "shtick" done by comedian Art Metrano.

It would begin by Tom singing "Da... Da Dada... Dada Dada" in some sequence that would go on and on and on while he performed his "magic." This "magic" included clicking his fists together and making his index fingers first "appear" and then "disappear."

Then there were the index fingers and thumbs forming circles and somehow "magically" interlocking, only coming apart when "hidden" behind his head!

Also included was taking his index fingers and first closing one ear and then both, bringing the "Da... Da Dada... Dada Dada" from soft to silent. And then, he would reverse this by suddenly removing both fingers so that we could continue to be amused or annoyed or both by the "Da" musical cadence. Eventually a lighter would appear and Tom would wave it back and forth, finally "hiding" it behind one hand, flicking it on with the other, and then dramatically removing his hand to show us how it had become "magically" lit!

The concluding "trick" involved Tom removing his jacket and slowly lowering it to the floor so that he could "make" one of his lower legs "disappear!" We could see this amazing feat (feet) occur as he brought the jacket up revealing a missing leg!! He only had the one he was standing on!!!

I knew I had to share this reflection when Bev told me to "knock off the Da... Da Dada... Dada Dada stuff" and my seven-year-old granddaughter, Elianna, hounded me to show her the "magic" involved with this! No wonder all ages were entertained by... Tom's "Magic." And they still are!!

"U Turn"

Sometimes, as you know, something only becomes humorous way after it happens. This is the case with this incident.

In Arkport, Terry and I would meet once a week at 6:30 am for Bible reflection and prayer before we went to work.   As I recall we alternated between the parsonage and his apartment. He lived between our house and the church building. On one occasion, we had just met at Terry's place and I remembered I needed to swing the car around and stop back at our house so that I could take out the trash- it was pickup day.

I dashed out to our Chocolate Colored Dodge Aries Station Wagon parked along the curb on West Main Street. A dusting of snow had occurred so everything was white. I thought I looked carefully before I started into a U turn when suddenly this grill appeared and BANG!! I had turned into an oncoming white Agway

Van. Fortunately, it hit behind where I was sitting but it did some serious damage to the car.

Exiting the driver's seat, the first thing I saw was a big slab of brown body filler, it had been dislodged and slid off the side of the car exposing dented metal from a previous owner's mishap. The car was so shoved in from the post behind the front seat to the back end that the Agway driver had to help me pull the fender away from the tire so that I could drive home.

Not only was I stunned by what had happened but I remember being extremely embarrassed as all these kids walked by on their way to school having just witnessed pastor Jeff demolish his car. I drove into our driveway and "hid" the car in our garage out of sight from those gawkers. And then I staggered into the kitchen, stammered something to Bev about an accident and told her to look at the car. In our 40 years of marriage, I have only heard her use this expression two or three times and this was one of them as I heard her exclaim, "OH MY GOD!"

THE "AX HANDLE AWARD"

We met Don the day we moved into the Arkport Parsonage. He and Dave, both south of six feet tall, arrived to help us with getting stuff off the U Haul I had driven up from seminary (with a stop at Bev's parents where we picked up more furniture). I gained a new appreciation of compacted strength when these two height-challenged men picked up Bev's piano like it was a piece of Styrofoam and took it from truck to the Living Room. This marked the beginning of a wonderful relationship with both men and their families.

But the focus of this reflection is Don and his family. Bev and I developed a comfortable and sometimes hilarious connection with Don and his wife, Lucy, over the eleven years we spent there. Lucy was a huge help in assisting me to get my office set up and my filing system going. She had a knack for picking up the way I thought to the extent that I turned over to her for filing, items I found in newspapers and books that could serve as future sermon illustrations.

Don made me laugh when he would ask me this question after delivering one of my sermons: "Now, what was that ($25) word you used?!" Being fresh out of seminary, I was determined to let the congregation know just how theologically erudite I was! The Lord used Don, and others, to remind me that I was there to communicate His love and truth instead of trying to impress with MY "greatness."

One of the more memorable and humorous incidents involved what I will call, "Don's Shortcut." We had traveled into Rochester to eat at Red Lobster. It was about a sixty-mile drive one way. Well, on the way back, Don suggested a shortcut. We started out on paved road but were soon on a dirt road that narrowed as we got deeper and deeper into some woods. Finally, it became a rutted, muddy path full of water-filled craters. I finally exclaimed, "This can't be right!" Somehow by backing up and finding a place to turn around, we made it out of this boondoggle.

The "Ax Handle Award" I received as we prepared to move from Arkport to Barker symbolizes the hilarity that marked my friendship with Don. A few years before I had volunteered to help Don split the wood he used to burn in the stove that helped heat the home.

This wood-splitting venture was short circuited by me breaking two sledge hammer handles on wedges I was using and then an ax handle on a chunk of wood! Accuracy was more difficult than I anticipated in my taking those mighty windmill swings!!

For some reason, he did not respond positively when I offered to help him split wood after that. He just... laughed.

So, Don thought it appropriate to recognize and "honor" my wood-splitting gone bad. The Ax Handle Award was really a repurposed baseball trophy. It contained the figure of a baseball player who had just hit a home run mounted on a base with the words punched into stamp metal, "Ax Handle Award."

"Hot Wheels"

When we were preparing to move after eleven unforgettable years in Arkport there was one thing I dreaded doing but it had to be done - at least in MY mind. It involved going into the basement and into the unfinished crawl space to retrieve items out of the heating duct work.

You see, Jed not only loved anything that moved, particularly his matchbox cars, but almost nothing topped hearing them bing-bang-bong down the furnace duct out of his room. He would take off the heating or cold-air return cover and send these little replicas flying. I imagine this entertained his little sister, Jeanna, as well.

Running out of cars never bothered him. There were other worthy small objects to be found. He even created a little ditty that he chanted: "a little boy... dropped his hammer... down the pipe, pipe, pipe, pipe."

Well, I always wondered where and how far these things had gone through the duct. So, as I mentioned in the beginning, I went into the basement crawl space under the house. It was a warm June day and the floor was dirt and I had to sit and pull apart the duct coming down out of his room. (Jed's room was upstairs and as far away from the furnace as you could get.) I can tell you that it did not go as smoothly as I had hoped. Maybe Jeanna DID get a choice word or two from me....

I managed to find a few cars and other objects in that duct work but the thing that amazed me the most was the match box racing car that had apparently zoomed-bing-bang-bonged it's way all the way to   the furnace! Jed, the Honda Tech, is still "playing" with cars.

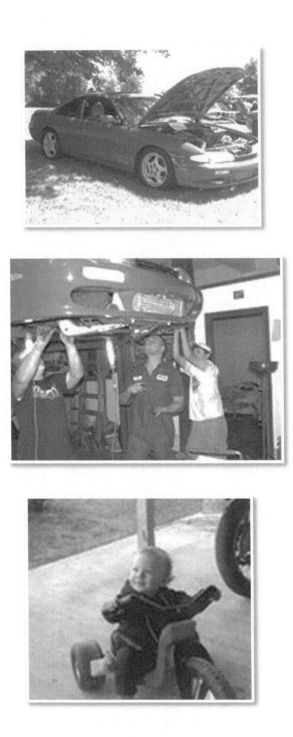

BARKER FAITH

1987 – 1991

"VANISHING SHOES"

My biggest regret in serving as a pastor was that I was only able to serve the Barker: Faith congregation for four of my 33 years of full time pastoral ministry. I had intended to stay at least 10 years and I declared that to the folks more than once. But then the Bishop asked me to serve as a District Superintendent. *That chapter is for later.*

After eleven wonderful years in Arkport we knew the Lord had led us to a community and church full of people wanting to grow and laugh! I discovered this quickly. At one of my first Administrative Board meetings, where I was looking to listen and suggest direction when needed, I took off my shoes. I wanted to get comfortable for this meeting that would be longer than future meetings (ha-ha). I heard many nuances about the life and needs of the church, including how far behind we were in our budget. I had no doubt this would be changed and it was, during the next four years.

It was a great meeting full of interaction and laughter. My laughter ended when after adjournment I couldn't find my shoes! "What's going on?" I thought as I first felt with my feet and then began looking under the table.

They were nowhere to be found, until the Treasurer presented them to me! There was great guffawing as I was "baptized" into a church culture I would come to love.

"CHIGAR SHMOKIN BOOSHER"

In the Barker congregation, there was a lovable couple, small of stature and of strong opinion. I spent some entertaining times visiting with and getting to know Oscar and Mildred. I can picture Oscar's sagging jowls shaking as he would express his view of this or that happening in the life of the church... or world. He made me burst into laughter one day with this statement: "I've liked every one of our pastors, except for that "**chigar shmokin boosher**!" At least that's the way I remember it.

Oscar was referring to a pastor who evidently had not been as discreet as he should have been about his smoking and drinking habits. What really bothered Oscar was that this pastor had been seen multiple times in one of Barker's two or less bars tipping a few and lighting up a stogie.

Well, as time would have it, years after serving the Barker congregation and with more discreetness I would enjoy an occasional cigar with a glass of beer or wine. This was usually with a friend or two in the congregation I was serving. Bev though, never let me forget Oscar's hilarious description of that former Barker pastor as she called me - and even still calls me - a

"Chigar shmokin boosher!"

"SARAH"

B arker: Faith had what I will call a Funny Bone Culture. Once people knew that my family and I loved being there they came out of the woodwork with their wackiness. There was Richard who told me every Sunday as I waited with the choir to process into the sanctuary to "break a leg." LeRoy and I soon enough realized that we both loved Oreo cookies. Silas enjoyed stopping by the office during the week for a laugh. Jim delighted in goofy gifts on special occasions. I could go on and on but maybe the nuttiest was Sarah.

Sarah made me laugh so many times with her "suggestions." One of them was that I figure out a way to make a grand entrance into the sanctuary on Sunday by sliding down a wire that ran from near an entrance to the platform area. There were others but the best was connected with a Christmas Tree Ornament she gave us our first year there.

We have been given several exceptional ornaments over the years but this has always been my favorite. I can't wait to find and hang it each year when we put up our tree. She had handcrafted it out of Popsicle Sticks, given it a festive look and beautifully written on it. It was a sled and it came with this note: "Just a little memento of your first year in Barker. You can go belly flop on this sled in your driveway when we get snow." HAHAHA!"

"CHRISTMAS FIREWORKS!"

Our Christmas celebrations in Barker were always marked by a fresh telling of the birth of Christ. A woman by the name of Eileen wrote and created these pageants by using Scripture and a cast made up of our children and youth. One of these included unintended fireworks.

The congregation had assembled with anticipation in the air. Mary and Joseph had taken their places behind the manger containing baby Jesus. The little Shepherds, with their crooks, were making their way into this scene with their bleating "sheep" children on all fours with sheep hats. They were followed by Wise Men/Women bearing gifts, dressed in fine robes, wearing gold paper crowns. This entourage had to negotiate a path between candelabras, providing most of the light.

Well, one of the Shepherds got too close to a candelabra and his headdress burst into flames. Everyone watching sat in shock, including the pastor (me). Before anyone could act, one of the youth, playing a Wise Man, calmly took two steps, snatched the flaming turban off the head off the unsuspecting Shepherd threw it on the floor and stomped out the fire. All of this happened without the flow of the pageant being broken as they say, the show went on!

The shock initially experienced by the congregation was followed by sighs of relief and disbelief that our kids could continue as though nothing happened. Of course, we could laugh afterwards, knowing that no one was injured, nothing got burned except for a slightly scorched Shepherd's hat, and that we had witnessed a most unforgettable and fresh presentation of the coming of Christ into the world, including Christmas fireworks! (Eileen swore that this was NOT in her script!)

JOY!

Our youngest, Joy Evelyn, was born while I was serving Barker: Faith. She came as a delightful surprise. Bev had told the doctor that she wanted to have her before she turned 42 (I would be 44). As it turned out Joy was delivered the day before Bev's birthday! I said to the doctor right after the delivery, "Well, Doc, you did it!" To which he responded, "What?" I reminded him of Bev's request and he kind of smiled - he didn't remember.

So, Joy is our Barker Baby. Jed and Jeanna, our Arkport Babies! I thought about the name "Joy" when I bought a stole to wear for special occasions - baptisms and weddings in particular. Joy was almost a year old when I purchased this special worship wear. She was just starting to say words like "Mama" and "Dad...da." I cooked up a plan to wear the stole for the first time and incorporate baby Joy into the Children's Time during the service. I was excited about showing off this new stole with the word "Joy" on it while holding Joy on my lap and having her utter her new and few words!

Well, everything went as planned until I asked Joy to "say something." Joy just looked at me and then at them and sat there mute. I could not get her to utter one word! As you can imagine, the congregation got quite a hoot out of the whole thing as I sat there, with the children gathered around me, red faced and trying to come up with something to say myself!

(It is quite a coincidence that last summer, on the 25th anniversary of purchasing that stole, I wore it as

I officiated at Joy's best friend's wedding. And Joy was there serving as a bridesmaid).

"PUSHING BUTTONS"

This reflection will serve to transition from Barker to the Olean District. I have Bev's permission to share this story.

I mentioned in another reflection that there were only two things - objects - I can ever recall Bev throwing at me. I described the frozen aluminum wrapped loaf of Banana Bread that came my way in that vignette. Well, this is the story of the other flying object.

Let's face it, in most marriages spouses learn certain buttons they can push if they want to really frustrate their partner. In the Barker parsonage, we had a spacious master bedroom that accommodated Bev's sewing machine, etc. She had gotten into the habit of collecting spare buttons by putting them into a glass Gerber baby food jar. We had a lot of them around having two and then three little ones.

One day we got into a disagreement about something in the bedroom and I would not let up expressing my point of view (which of course was probably wrong). Bev was getting more and more aggravated and I started to think it was funny. I was smiling and laughing when I saw that Bev was fed up with my provocation. This became apparent when she reached for the baby jar full of buttons sitting next to the sewing machine.

I knew I had limited time to take evasive action - to protect myself from incoming - so I ran for the master bathroom. I jumped through the doorway and yanked the pocket door closed just before impact. That baby jar full of buttons slammed into the lower part of that door with a "KABOOM!"

I slid the door back enough to get out and then partially closed it and we both saw the damage - there was a noticeable dent in the bedroom side of that hollow core door! We were too embarrassed to tell anyone except for one couple in the congregation with whom we were especially close. I don't recall how many more months or years we were in Barker after this incident. Since the door stayed in the wall most of the time we forgot about it.

Later, we heard that the dent was discovered when some folks went in to spruce up the parsonage for the next pastor and family. This group included our friends. Someone asked: "Hey, how did the door get caved in here?!" To which our friends, bursting into fiendish laughter, spilled the beans about the baby jar full of buttons. I guess the whole crew got quite a kick out of it... thankfully!

THE OLEAN DISTRICT
1991 - 1995

"STRING MUSIC"

In my fourth year in Barker the Bishop asked me to consider becoming a District Superintendent.

After prayerful consideration and talking it over with Bev I said "yes." Our time in Barker was wonderful and I regret only being able to serve there for four years. In July of 1991 I became the Superintendent of what was called the Olean District. It comprised an area Inclusive of Salamana, NY, in the West and Hornell, NY, in the east and spanned from the Pennsylvania State line in the South to a zigzag line that included Springville, NY and other communities towards Buffalo.

My responsibility was to oversee sixty United Methodist Churches as well be a pastor to pastors and their families. Many of these churches were in rural settings or villages. I largely enjoyed this time and felt it a privilege to be in this unique pastoral role.

You can imagine that in the first few months I was very busy orienting myself to the complexities of this ministry. There was an office to organize, churches to attend to and pastors to check on. While I was doing these sorts of things Bev was getting things settled in the District Parsonage and riding herd on our three children.

I have her permission to tell about an incident that occurred during these first months. Bev has a beautiful Baldwin piano that was moved from parsonage to parsonage and sits in our Living Room today. She is an accomplished pianist and has found opportunities to play wherever we have lived. Each time the piano has been moved it has needed to be tuned. It was no different when we moved into this home. One day when I was off somewhere Bev had someone come to tune the piano. When I got home, she said "You are not going to believe what happened!" She then told me that after the piano tuner had left and she sat down to play one of the strings still was not right. It was the G string!

It took her a while to think about how she was going to call this guy and tell him that her "G string was not right and he was going to have to come back and fix it."

"We still laugh about that and his response. He told her that he "was sorry and that he would be right over!"

"EARL'S GARAGE"

There were two things I discovered soon after beginning my appointment as a District Superintendent on the Olean District. The first was that the vast majority of the 46 pastors who were serving appointments were men and women who were blooming where they were planted. These precious pastors had a deep affection for their congregations and communities. And they were focused on loving people into the Kingdom of God.

The other thing I learned was that just like everywhere, there was a rich fabric of colorful personalities making up the communities where United Methodist Churches were located. Nowhere was this more evident than in a place over towards the eastern side of the District where Pastor Dave served. Dave had a wacky sense of humor and made sure I knew about anything that occurred in his church and community that tickled the funny bone.

There are several stories I could share but one in particular stands out.

Pastor Dave described an auto repair business in this small village known as Earl's Garage. Earl, the owner, was elderly and almost blind. His son had mostly taken over the business but his dad still came to the shop every day. Earl was quick to dispense advice to this younger grease monkey. In the colder months, he and some of his old cronies would gather around a pot-bellied stove to drink coffee and swap yarns. I guess many of the stories were of the hard to believe type and snorts and guffaws punctuated the conversation.

The hilarious part was the sign that was posted between the big garage door and the smaller "people" door. All who entered Earl's Garage were greeted by these words:

IF ASSHOLES COULD FLY
THIS PLACE WOULD BE
AN AIRPORT!!

"TICKED OFF"

One of my responsibilities as a Superintendent was to conduct annual meetings-called Charge or Church Conferences - in the churches of the District. I mentioned in the two previous reflections that there were sixty churches and 46 pastors. A few pastors served two churches, this is called a two-point charge. I tried to be present in every church at least once a year.

One night I traveled to one of the smaller churches of the district for its annual meeting. It was part of a two-point charge. As in all of these meetings, officers for the next year were to be elected and a budget adopted. It was extremely unusual for the attendance at one of these meetings to match that of a typical Sunday morning. However, in this case it was close. Only a few were missing from the normal 35-40.

The folks were extremely upset with their pastor and cited several ways he was failing them. Some of what they said appeared to be valid reasons for why this pastor didn't fit well in their church. They concluded their litany of his deficiencies by demanding his immediate removal!!

I remember standing before them and telling them that this could not happen. It was November and the time for changing pastors was July. I urged them to consider the ramifications for their pastor and his family and reminded them that this was not just my decision to make. The Bishop made appointments with the District Superintendents providing counsel. I assured them that I would bring their concerns to one of our bi-monthly meetings and we would see what could be done looking towards July.

Then I brought their budget before them. Now they had put this budget together after what I am sure was much detailed and careful consideration. Well, they DEFEATED IT!! Here was a congregation voting down its own budget because I would not agree to their demand! I found a stool and sat down. I then informed them that I was just going to sit there until someone made a Motion to Reconsider.

After some tense moments, someone made the motion and the budget was adopted!

As it unfolded it was far from humorous. But by the time I arrived back at the district parsonage I was finding it comedic. When I walked into the house laughing Bev asked me what was so funny. I told her about how I had run into a group of folks who were so ticked off that they voted down their own budget!! HAHAHA!

"BAG LADY"

This reflection is about neighbors. In most of the places I served there were unique and wonderful neighbors. In many cases I have enjoyed giving them nicknames. Our next-door neighbor in Arkport was Jerry "The Mechanic." In his spare time, he seemed to be working on a bike, motorcycle or his car. In fact, Jed, as a toddler, used to like to sit in the grass beside Jerry's driveway and watch him. One day, Jerry said to me, "Your son is unusually fascinated by what I am doing." Then there was Don "The Manicurist." His property was immaculate and he loved to walk around his lawn barefoot in the summer with a cup of coffee admiring his work. Finally, there was Fritz "The Neighborhood Philosopher." As I walked up West Avenue towards the church building Fritz would often be sitting on his porch and sometimes would invite me to "come up and have coffee." He had an opinion about almost everything and "logic" to back it up!

Barker was unique because the parsonage was located on the church property and there were no close neighbors. In Penfield, although the parsonage was also on church property, we had some neighbors who I may describe later. And in Canandaigua there was an apartment building next to the parsonage on Main Street where a family lived who I will focus on in a later reflection. Even where we live now, in retirement, there is a neighbor who is notable for his accumulating gadgets to "make things easier." In our seven years here it has not been uncommon for me to hear a whir, buzz, whine or roar and look out to discover Gary has acquired a new gizmo to edge the driveway, trim bushes, clean up the lawn, remove leaves from eve's troughs, etc. I call him Gary "Gadget."

The neighbor with a Jeff-given nickname who I laugh about the most is one of our neighbors in Allegheny, where the district parsonage was located. We had colorful neighbors on both sides and across the street but the one who most lent herself to being described lived across our backyard in a cul-de-sac. Marian was a really nice woman who had a husband

and two teenage daughters. Her home and property were attractive and she was a woman who caught one's eye. She was always nicely dressed and her hair well coifed. Except for one wintry day.

I was standing at the kitchen sink sipping my first cup of coffee and looking out the window I almost blew coffee all over. I gulped and then burst out laughing and told Bev to come and "check this out." There was a person who had to be Marian, coming out of a side garage door, with a stocking cap pulled down over her head, in a long house coat, wearing tall rubber boots. She was carrying a bag of trash in each hand and was heading for the curb. Immediately she earned the nickname, Marion "Bag Lady!" The only thing that would make it funnier would be if I could use her last name.

"MIMIC"

One of the things I enjoyed the most about being a District Superintendent was the privilege of helping congregations celebrate special occasions such as 100 years of ministry in a community. Many times, I could take my family with me. It was also great to be able to use a sermon more than once!

It was on one such occasion that a crazy thing happened. My family and I traveled to the Arcade United Methodist Church so that I could help them celebrate persons who had achieved 50 years of membership. I had used a sermon titled "Beggar at the Gate" several times.

The Scripture text was Acts 3:1-10 - Peter and John raise up a man lame from birth. My major illustration was an experience I had while in Seoul, South Korea. Our tour bus had to wait at the gate of an immense parking lot for the largest Methodist Church in the world. A legless beggar who had scooted into the entrance had to be picked up and moved!

I could preach this sermon extemporaneously because of multiple uses. I didn't even think about how similar my gestures, words and phrases were each time I shared this. It went well as I unleashed "Beggar at the Gate" once again. We congratulated these long-term members and gave them nice certificates. I was basking in glory when Bev approached me after the benediction.

She proceeded to tell me that eleven- or twelve-year-old son Jed, who had heard me preach this sermon three times, was sitting back in the pew with his sisters mimicking my gestures and lip-syncing my words! Bev had spent some tense and embarrassing moments trying to get him to STOP! She had not only spoken sternly to him but also used her arms to keep him from mocking his "esteemed" preacher Dad, the Olean District Superintendent.

When she described what he was doing during the sermon I was only glad I didn't catch him at it. I would have lost it! Can you imagine me appearing to find a legless beggar funny, suddenly bursting into laughter in the middle of my sermon?! Picturing this makes me laugh out loud today.

"CAT TALES"

These reflections must include a focus on cats. From the beginning of full time pastoral ministry until well into retirement we had a cat. This was mainly due to the women in the family who insisted we have one. There were four cats who, in my mind, distinguished themselves for both their longevity and their personalities. Also, each had a memorable moniker (I admit helping with the naming).

"Little Turkey" - "Turk" - was our first cat. This was our Arkport cat. You will see below that among other things "Little Turkey" liked to play the piano! The last and fourth cat was "Lucky Lady" ,"Lucky." This was our Penfield/Canandaigua/Fairport cat. We acquired "Lucky" when someone dropped her off at the Penfield Church doors and we dubbed her lucky to have found a nice home.

My second name for "Lucky Lady" was "Barf." She had a habit during her twelve-year existence of spitting up food that (thankfully) had just been eaten. According to the Veterinarian she had a smaller than normal esophagus. She was our people cat and is pictured below.

In between "Little Turkey" and "Lucky Lady" we had two other long-lived cats. One was "Mr. Maxwell" - "Max" - and the other was "Burkatroid" or "Troidy Boy." I don't remember much about "Mr. Maxwell" but "Burkatroid" gave us some laughable memories. A couple of those trace back to the district.

By the way, "Troidy Boy" got his name from the Snagglepuss character on the Yogi Bear Show. I came up with this name. It was a takeoff from Snagglepuss saying "Heavens to Murgatroyd." I used to say, "Heavens to Murgatroyd, if it isn't Burkatroid!" I am sure this makes total sense to anyone with my wackiness.

One day when I was in the backyard of the district parsonage, a little rabbit made the poor choice of hopping into eye-shot of "Burkatroid." There ensued a chase that made us all laugh. I didn't want to watch our cat catch and crunch down that poor little bunny, especially with the kids looking on. So, I began chasing "Burkatroid" while he was in pursuit of the rabbit.

The three of us went zigzagging across the yard with me yelling something like "STOP IT NOW... GET AWAY FROM IT!" I did manage to prevent what would have been a... hare raising incident!

On another occasion "Troidy Boy" was chasing a chipmunk across the front porch when one of us opened the door and in they both came! The chipmunk, running for its life, darted behind a curtain in the living room, behind the couch, into another room and disappeared. This happened right after dinner and we all had places to be. So as frustrating as it was we left the house with the chipmunk in it, praying that "Burkatroid" would make it

disappear by the time we came home.

We never again saw that chipmunk. And I will never forget that cat, whose name was derived from a cartoon character saying: "Heavens to Murgatroyd!" Why... it was "Burkatroid!"

"BEER PARTY!"

One of my major missions as a District Superintendent was to bring pastors and their families together for encouragement and fun. We called ourselves the "Parsonage People." Each year I tried to make our Parsonage People Christmas party something special. We alternated between an adult party in a nice restaurant and one that was family oriented in one of the churches of the district.

It was during one of our family gatherings in a village church that a most hilarious thing happened. We enjoyed a wonderful meal in the fellowship hall. Then the adults adjourned to the sanctuary for a brief worship experience. A highlight was to be the ministry of a fledgling bell choir. This music group had been formed within the last few months and unfortunately was missing two or three members. Now anyone knows that even for an experienced bell choir, missing ringers can make a performance extremely tenuous.

Well, this choir tried to play a familiar Christmas song but it didn't take long before something didn't sound right. Missing ding dongs started leading to confusion. The conductor tried to get the members who had shown up back on track. First, she became visibly more demonstrative in her baton use. It didn't help. Then she began stomping the beat on the floor. It still didn't help. Finally, she waved "CUT!" She then turned to the audience - us - and with a forced smile, said they would try it again. It still didn't help as it all broke into a cacophony!

I can tell you I was sitting there with Bev doing everything I could to contain myself. I didn't know HOW I was going to keep from just bursting into uncontrolled laughter!!! I kept looking down and Bev had a hold of my arm. I even prayed something like "Lord don't let this happen!" I mean I was the District Superintendent who had in some sense orchestrated this event and I absolutely COULD NOT break down this way!!

Thank the Lord I found relief when suddenly I saw a half a bottle of beer under the pew in front of us. It was unbelievable - miraculous! The Lord must have providentially planned my relief hours before. I released some of my pent-up hilarity as I pointed at that beer bottle. After the service, I mentioned it to the pastor who was tremendously embarrassed. She said they had found the town drunk sleeping in a back pew earlier in the day and thought they had cleaned up the sanctuary. Sometime later, as I prepared to leave the district, I was given a card by the district pastors. Underneath the words inside the card which said, "Did we have a good time, or what?" she wrote: "Yeah, especially the beer party!"

"STRIPPER"

This reflection will serve to transition from the district to serving as the pastor of the Penfield United Methodist Church. During my fourth year of serving as a superintendent, I began to feel that I should return to a local church pastoral role. Bev had to deal with everything while I was out many nights visiting churches. And the night travel to churches and back was beginning to wear on me.

So, the Cabinet (Bishop and other superintendents) appointed me to Penfield in the Rochester area.

As we prepared to move we had a couple of pieces of furniture that needed to be refinished. I knew just the person to do this. He was married to a pastor on the district who I had to defend and counsel on more than one occasion. It was reported to me that this pastor had gotten into the habit of kicking off her shoes during worship and dancing around the chancel area (the platform in the front of the sanctuary). The folks were not used to this behavior and many were upset. So, they called me in to discuss this.

Let me say that this behavior was not as outlandish to me as one might think. My wife, Bev, and I consider ourselves "Methacostals" - Methodists with a Pentecostal dynamic. We had - and have - been in many settings where we have seen this. But it was obviously inappropriate in a typical United Methodist Church and so I agreed with the congregation that this needed correction. I engaged this "dancing pastor" in more than one conversation and she was reluctant but willing to alter her behavior. We left the district within months of these goings on with newly refinished furniture, courtesy of her husband, the expert in furniture repair, refurbishing and refinishing.

Well, during the first two years in Penfield, I received a phone call from the pastor of a Pentecostal-Charismatic Church in Wellsville, NY. This community was on my district and we had gotten to know this pastor through a friend of ours who attended the church. He told me that the reason for his call was that the "dancing pastor" was seeking credentialing by his

Fellowship. I told him that I was glad to hear this and that she probably would fit better in that body because of her theological-liturgical leanings.

I saw my opportunity to "jerk his chain" and so I told him, "But you know her husband is a Professional Stripper." There was silence on his end and I was enjoying the thought of Mason picturing the spouse of the "dancing pastor" taking the stage as a Chippendale. Finally, he responded, "YOU'RE KIDDING!" To which I said, laughing of course, "He strips furniture for a living." The last words I remember him saying after a silent pause were, "DON'T DO THAT TO ME!" I never knew what happened to "The Dancing Pastor" or her "Stripper" husband.

PENFIELD

1995 - 2004

"HYENA"

I t was within the first years of an eventful nine year stay in Penfield that my friendship with Mark began. A group of men traveled to what was then called Rich Stadium in Orchard Park, NY, for a "Promise Keepers Rally." This was a two-day event with a focus on challenging men to become better husbands and fathers through an ignited faith in Jesus Christ. At that point Mark's family attended Penfield United Methodist Church regularly. I occasionally saw him and so was delighted when he decided to join the group attending the Rally.

Mark is quite a sports enthusiast and was very familiar with Rich Stadium because it was the home of the Buffalo Bills football team. On the first night of the Rally, the Lord used the preaching of a pastor from Indianapolis to convict Mark of his need for salvation. When this pastor, whose message was full of sports images, gave his invitation to make Jesus Savior and Lord, Mark shot up and headed down from our seating in an upper deck to the floor of the stadium. I was amazed and immediately followed him so that I could be of support in any way I could.

Mark committed his life to the Lord on that day in the late 90's and has been a disciple of Christ since. Throughout the rest of my nine years in Penfield, Mark and I met on an almost weekly basis for a time of mutual faith strengthening. I called this "discipling" and was involved in this kind of relationship everywhere I served as a local church pastor.

It was during the first time that we met, in my office in the church, that a most unusual thing happened. I was prepared to launch into this exciting and serious venture with discipling materials and my Bible when Mark arrived. Then ensued fifteen minutes or more of laughter.... I have never had this experience before or since, seriously!! I COULD NOT STOP LAUGHING! Every time I tried to begin I broke into laughter. If I spoke a word - or began a sentence - I broke into almost uncontrollable laughter. There was no real reason for this other than that I found anything and everything funny.

Mark just sat there and laughed at my strange behavior. We hardly knew one another at that point and here I was "The Discipling Pastor" and all I could do was laugh like a hyena!! I even tried to apologize more than once and before I could get the words, "I am so sorry" out of my mouth, I broke into laughter. We BOTH had tears in our eyes. That day I discovered that I had met someone with a kindred spirit - who had as jocular a dynamic to his personality as me. To this day, it doesn't take much to bring out of both us that lurking... Hyena!

"THE INCREDIBLE ENLARGING MACHINE"

In Penfield, there was - and still is - an annual "Talent Night" or "Talent Show." This was very like Arkport, where I served first. There were a variety of "acts" including sweet children singing, playing an instrument or engaging in drama of some kind and adults doing serious or nutty "shticks."

One of the two most notable acts in which I participated included Mark (mentioned in an earlier reflection) and me doing a Blues Brothers Rendition. I went to the famous Arlene's Costume Store and rented appropriate attire for this and the song and dance we did was a crazy impression of Jake and Elwood.

The other act was something our family put together. We called it, "The Incredible Enlarging Machine." We got this idea from a hilarious performance by Joyce Osborn and her husband, Carlton, in an Arkport Talent Night. I will attempt to describe how it unfolded.

We found a refrigerator container and opened it up to form three sides of a "Machine." We then cut large slots with flaps in the front and side of the box and decorated the whole thing to look machine-like. We were able to get a tape of machine sounds - Bev says it was sound effects from "Music Machine," a kid's musical. Eleven or twelve-year-old, Jeanna, was decked out in a lab coat and stood in the front of the "Machine." The rest of us, Jed, Joy, Bev and I were stationed inside and made sure the "Machine" functioned properly.

As the "Incredible Enlarging Machine" cranked up with whirs, hums and clanks, Jeanna would push something very small through the side slot and we would send out through the front slot a much larger version of the same item. It had become incredibly ENLARGED! A tiny spring was fed into the "Machine" and out came a garage door coil. A Beanie Baby became a large stuffed animal. A matchbox car was turned into a large Barbie Doll car. And on and on it went.

The climax was reached when five or six-year-old Joy, who had somehow appeared at Jeanna's side, was "fed" through the side slot. This was followed by a dramatic pause with an increase in the volume of machine sounds. Suddenly, only in my first year of ministry in Penfield, I came busting through the front of the machine, knocking the whole thing down. I was dressed only in a diaper made with a sheet and a T shirt! I was holding a gallon milk jug in one hand with a baby bottle nipple taped on the top! I made a beeline up the middle aisle of the sanctuary as a stunned audience sat in disbelief before bursting into laughter.

That night, if they hadn't discovered it before, they became profoundly aware of the wackiness of their new pastor... and his family!!!

"WHY IT'S THE PASTOR..."

Progressing into our nine year stay in Penfield we got to know our neighbors on Baird Road. The guy next door liked to amp up his music when he was grilling or just hanging out on a day off. He loved Steve Winwood. The man kitty corner from us, across the street, got AMPED UP over teenager, Jed, playing his music too loud when he was working on his truck or car in the garage. One day he came over and swore at him - I spoke to Jed about it and then tried to calm down the upset neighbor. The lady directly across from the parsonage drove the same circuit of streets at least twice a day for some unknown reason. There were two hippie-like women who lived next to the "Circuit Driver." Just south of them was a younger family who we tried to get along with but it was difficult. The man of the house had a hair trigger - it didn't take much to provoke him. He yelled at Jed for mowing the lawn after dinner and told me that a light pole that had been put up at the entrance to the church parking lot was "Butt Ugly!" I laughed over that one!! We appreciated in every way we could all of these people. Then there were Mel and Ruth.

Mel and Ruth were a gracious older couple who loved the Lord and enjoyed life. They lived directly across the street from the church building and property and Mel was the watchdog of the parking lot, which was largely hidden from view. He would call me, even at midnight, if he saw some suspicious vehicle go behind the church into the lot. "Hey, Pastor," he would say, "something might be going on back there." Mel had what I would call a good-natured goofiness. He just blurted out stuff and could bend your ear for a long time. In the words of a friend of mine, Mel could make "a long story longer!" He befriended Jed at a critical time and the two made quite a pair - "Old Mel" and teenager Jed hanging out. Sweet Ruth just rolled with all of this.

One Halloween I decided to prank Mel and Ruth. I covered my face with Clown White and put a pair of heart-printed boxer shorts on my head (like a chef's hat). I wore a long coat and boots. In my mind, I was completely disguised - there was NO way they could tell who I was! I took a garbage bag to their house and when Ruth came to the front door with a bowl of candy I spoke in a gruff voice unlike my own and made grunting noises. I first took a couple of pieces of candy and then grabbed the whole bowl from her and dumped it in my bag. About that time Ruth said, "Why it's the pastor from up the street." I couldn't believe it... and still can't!

Mel and Ruth still live across from the church property on Baird Road in Penfield. Mel still watches the property. And he still bends anyone's ear he can. In fact, he just bent mine the other day at the chicken barbecue on the front lawn of the church. Sweet Ruth eventually joined him and we had a nice reunion. I STILL can't believe it!!!!

"SANTA CLOD"

Penfield United Methodist Church has a Christian Preschool that has grown over the years. It was started before I became the pastor and is thriving today. Each year on a Saturday morning in December the preschool hosts a Breakfast with Santa. One year while I was the pastor they were desperate for someone to play Santa and I reluctantly agreed to do this. I was not very comfortable with the idea of having to become The Claus with all the "ho ho ho's" and kiddy conversation involved. I was told to be at the church a half hour before I was to assume this character in full costume. When I arrived, I was given a well-worn Santa suit and went into my office to change.

This began one of the most pressure packed and sweat producing half hours of my life. There were black spats to fit over shoes to simulate Santa boots. Immediately I went to work putting on the Santa pants. I soon discovered that the bottom of the pant legs would not fit over my tennis shoes. In fact, I got one pant leg stuck half way over my shoe and was hopping around the office on one leg until in my struggle I fell into a chair. I couldn't untie the shoe because it was up inside the pant leg. I began to sweat as I looked at the clock and realized my half hour was slipping away. After what seemed an eternity I managed to get the pant leg off the shoe. I then removed my shoes and put on the Santa pants.

About then it struck me that a Santa Claus wearing tennis shoes, even with black spats covering part of the tops, was going to look ridiculous. So, I made the decision to run over to the house and change into black dress shoes. Meanwhile the clock continued to tick and I still had to put on the rest of the outfit - padding, coat, curly beard, wig and hat. I managed to get back to my office with five minutes to spare.

I was putting on the padding and coat when a knock on my door occurred and someone asked, "Are you ready?" I said, "Not yet," as I continued wrestling with the costume. The beard was somewhat gnarly with an elastic band that had lost its elasticity. I had to tie it behind my head so that it would stay on my face.

I had no sooner secured it when there was another knock, "We need to begin." I stated that I was "almost ready" as I spun the wig on my head so that it looked right. A check in the mirror told me that I looked like I was wearing Albino Skunk Road Kill for hair but what could I do? I put on the hat and was out the door.

Breathing heavily and sweating profusely I headed up the hallway to the narthex where the crowd had gathered and the kids were lined up to sit on my knee. I had already noticed my glasses fogging up as I breathed through the beard. About that time, I felt like punching the guy who I was dressed to portray in his bowl full of jelly but could only force some "ho ho ho's" as I began my stint as... Santa Clod.

Addendum: Bev showed up as Mrs. Santa at the end and jumped into my lap, almost tipping us over backward and launching us out of the Santa Rocker!

"MAX'S PLACE"

I estimate that I have married something like 150 couples during the time I have been a pastor, including into retirement. I have always required at least conversations if not full-blown counseling sessions to help prepare them for this most intimate life-long commitment. There is one of these conversations/sessions that tops anything before or since for comedic value.

I shall call the couple involved, Rob and Katie. This happened during my nine years in Penfield. I resonated with Rob and Katie from the beginning of our journey towards marriage. I sensed a maturity about them, they both had a great sense of humor and they each seemed to take into their souls our time of preparation. In one of our meetings I asked what it was that they really valued about each other and then what it was about the other that really bugged them.

What they valued about each other was rich but somewhat similar to what I had heard shared by other couples. It was when we got into what bugged them about each other that I just lost it. For at least fifteen minutes or more, Katie went on a rant about Rob's dog, Max. Rob kind of smiled as she unrelentingly cited example after example of an Irish Setter (as I recall) who was TOTALLY OUT OF CONTROL!

"Rob's commands mean nothing! There is dog hair everywhere!! I can't sit on the couch without getting hair all over my clothes!! Max even sleeps with Rob! He needs to take him to Dog Obedience School...." On and on and on it went as I dissolved in a fit of laughter. Katie concluded this unabated venting with, "Rob might as well have a sign over the front door that says, 'MAX'S PLACE!'"

And THAT pretty much finished our time together because, for one thing, I could do nothing but howl. Rob DID get the message! I married them a few weeks later. Max was taken to dog obedience classes. They have two growing boys who are a delight to be around. Thankfully, I see them on a regular basis when we worship at Penfield UMC.

Occasionally, Rob and I will "knock the froth off a couple." Oh, and we still laugh over "the funniest premarital counseling session I ever had."

"SEPTIC DINING"

A Septic System had been installed for the new parsonage on Baird Road in Penfield. At that point, there was no sewer line coming down the road. A few years after our moving in a trench was blasted so that homes could be connected to the town system. I say "blasted" because there was a vein of Dolomite running through properties in that area. I remember someone coming before and after the blasting to make sure cracks had not occurred in the walls of our home.

When that line was installed the Trustees decided to attach the church building to it but not the parsonage. That was fine with us because the biannual cleaning of our septic tank was a seamless process and it was much less expensive than paying a sewer bill every month. The sequence of events went something like this. The "Honey Wagon" appeared and backed into our driveway, the "Dippers" located the septic tank cover, a large hose was dragged over their shoulders from truck to tank, a one to two-hour emptying began, and they were gone.

One year the wagon showed up in the late morning. I had come over for lunch and found the whole process fascinating. I chatted with the dippers as they positioned the hose and began cleaning out the tank. I couldn't imagine doing this for a living but was thankful for tough guys who do this necessary work. I kidded with them about sayings they could have printed on the side of their truck like, "Our business stinks but it's a honey of a job."

They humored me as they went about their work. They'd probably heard this one and other "waste" jokes a million times. I thought it was interesting that they were wearing white T shirts that didn't look particularly white. I doubted they bought them new with brown splotches all over them. There was one unforgettable thing that they did that still makes me chuckle.

It apparently was lunch time for them like it was for me. So, I watched in some disbelief as they got their lunch boxes out of the honey wagon, sat down beside the septic tank and had sandwiches! I have to admit I had a hard time eating my own sandwich that day... in the sanitized surroundings of my kitchen!

"WE SAW THAT DAD!"

I just reflected on how something can provoke a dumb decision, creating a less than proud moment, when I shared the story about "LiL Wayne." I gave myself permission to tell about one of those moments in my life as a pastor. It happened one day when I was on my way back to the parsonage from a "Y" workout.

Our home was located on the church property on Baird Road in Penfield. Unfortunately, Baird Road was used as a through street - a short cut - between major arteries north and south. The speed limit was 35 miles an hour but it was not uncommon for people cutting through to drive 50 miles an hour or more. It was a dangerous place for small children and teenagers walking or riding bikes since there were no sidewalks or even decent shoulders along the side of the road. On more than one occasion when I was doing yard work I yelled at these drivers to "SLOW DOWN!"

On the particular day to which I refer I had just made my turn from Atlantic Avenue onto Baird Rd. and was heading south towards the parsonage. It was about a third of a mile to the driveway. I had no sooner rounded the corner when a little red truck sped up behind me. I was deliberately (as always) driving about 35 miles an hour and could tell this driver wanted to go much faster. Even though there was a double solid yellow line down the middle of the road he was about to fly by me when I got mad enough to ease over the lines myself so that he could not pass. There followed an extremely frustrated guy in his little red truck.

When I reached our house I slowed down, signaled and slowly made the turn into our driveway. I was watching in my rear-view mirror to see what would happen and saw the truck pull over and stop. The driver appeared to exit and I was ready for a confrontation. So, I immediately got out of my car and headed down the driveway, pointing towards him. The words we exchanged were not very nice. I called him an "Idiot Brain" after he called me a name I will not mention, but it has the word "ass" in it.

Well, as I drew near he jumped in that little red truck and put the peddle to the metal. I was pretty hyped up when I turned around to walk to the garage. I hadn't even looked that way because of my intense focus in the other direction. I suddenly became aware that Penfield High School student, Jed, and another young man who was living with us, Tyrone, were sitting in lawn chairs in the garage and had seen the whole ridiculous incident unfold. I tried to pretend nothing had happened by suddenly - and hilariously - undergoing a complete change in my demeanor as I asked in a flat tone, "How's it going guys?"

Jed and Tyrone erupted, exclaiming, "WE SAW THAT, DAD! THAT GUY IS ONE OF OUR TEACHERS!!" Well, I was, as they say, had, by not only my two sons, but by the Lord! It was day that will go down in pastoral infamy, along with the phrase, "Idiot Brain!"

"LIL WAYNE"

In the Penfield congregation, there was a smallish but notable man who I will call "LiL Wayne." He is not to be confused with the "LiL Wayne" of rap and teeth grill fame. No, this LiL Wayne was a devotee of Jesus Christ and a dedicated church man. He impressed me with his gentle and fun-loving personality. And he relished calling to my attention something he had been thinking about... or treasured, like a couple of old cars he had restored.

This LiL Wayne had a diminutive wife and children and grandchildren who loved the Lord and some of them were involved in our Penfield church. In fact, they still are! And although Wayne has passed on, his wife is there almost every Sunday. He obviously spiritually influenced his family and his legacy is beautiful.

Well, one day while I was Wayne's pastor I caught something about him in our local paper. It indicated that he had been to an altercation and had gotten banged up! So, I called him to check on things and followed up with a visit. He told me that he had become completely fed up with people who thought his "No Outlet" street was a race track. So, he had decided to take action. A car had gone flying by his house and before this punk (my word) could turn around Wayne walked into the street, obstructing his attempt to zoom back! Standing in front of the car he then sprawled across the hood!!

The driver was so incensed that he got out and pulled Wayne off the front of his car and pushed him to the curb. Fortunately, he was not seriously hurt. His story elicited both a chuckle and some advice from me. I suggested that maybe he ought to let the police handle these kinds of things. With a feisty grin, he agreed.

I was reminded that there are always new and exciting things to learn about someone. I discovered that, in the words of Jim Croce, "You don't pull that mask off the old Lone Ranger and you don't mess around with... (Wayne)."

HAHAHA, I believe the Sheriff's Department increased its patrol in Lil Wayne's neighborhood, as much to insure his safety as anything else!!

"SQUIRMINATOR"

Bev's dad had made a birdfeeder which I put on a post and attached to a deck rail at the back of the parsonage. Almost immediately little thieves began stealing the bird seed. Squirrels decided it was an easy way to cop a meal. I tried everything to keep them out of the feeder. I greased the pole and watched one slide down. I trimmed tree branches back so they couldn't jump onto the top of the feeder. I put a large round piece of aluminum under the feeder to prevent them from coming up into it. But somehow those clever little rodents found a way to pilfer Bev's bird food. I told her several times that all she was doing was feeding the squirrels.

I had observed much of this relentless thievery from our master bedroom bathroom on the second floor of the parsonage and had had enough. I realized what a good angle I had from this viewpoint. So, as a last resort I decided to try shooting them off the top of the feeder. I purchased a 22 Rifle just like the one I grew up with - a single shot bolt action Savage - at Walmart. And for the next few weeks I was successful at popping one squirrel after another - seven in a row - off the birdfeeder from the window of our bathroom on the second floor. Incredibly, I never put a hole in the "squirrel feeder!" However, the eighth squirrel didn't pop off - it expired on the top of the feeder and bled down through it. My Terminator days ended with the demise of number eight. By then I had put a stop to this nuisance anyway, for the time being.

Some may question the safety and legality of this activity. Well, I was extremely careful about when I fired my gun. I made sure it was during a time when no one was around. There was nothing beyond our back yard but an empty parking lot and brush and woods. And I would shoot almost straight down from the second floor. As for legality, I was careful who I told. It was probably not going to be helpful or healthy to brag about being a Squirrel Terminator (Squirminator). People could have been discussing Pastor Jeff's arrest!

I DID share my action with a few friends and they will never let me forget it. For the past seventeen years

I have received a Squirrel Birthday Card from one couple. I guess these cards are limitless. And I have a T shirt that is at least twelve years old, given to me by a friend in the congregation. It has pictures of ten squirrel faces on it. Each face is mounted on what looks like a Wanted Poster. They have names like "Sammy Seeds," "Mickey Snake Eyes," "Jimmy the Mole," and "Lucky." The shirt reads: "Ten Most Wanted" for birdseed crimes - suspects are at large and considered to be a menace to backyard birdfeeders everywhere."'

These rodent robbers, just like the ones in my backyard, needed terminating. And I was the sly pastor to do it! Just call me "The Squirminator."

"RONE"

I mentioned Tyrone in a previous reflection. He gave me permission to tell this - his - story. I called him "Rone" and it is a nickname that has stuck since. Rone lived with us during his senior year in high school. His mom and sisters had moved from Penfield to Spencerport and he wanted to stay and finish school. We had gotten to know him before he moved into our home because of his friendship with Jed and Jeanna. He was a sharp young man with a keen wit and wacky sense of humor. He became like a second son to us and to this day he calls me "Pops", telling me that I am the closest thing he has, to a dad.

Rone's sense of humor has gotten him into a little trouble over the years but in the end people understand that he means no harm and for the most part they enjoy his wackiness. An instance I can think of since he graduated from high school was when he served in the Navy aboard the Air Craft Carrier, USS Theodore Roosevelt. Rone was an Aviation Boatswains Mate and a member of the crew who operated the

Catapult and the Arresting Gear. He helped launch planes from the carrier and then helped retrieve them. It was an extremely demanding and dangerous job and I am sure some comic relief was welcomed among the airmen. Rone was the man to help provide it. I have seen a video clip of him holding a Boom Box on his shoulder while Moon Walking across the empty flight deck. His superiors didn't find this activity particularly humorous, at least to his face. But I can see them busting a gut while they watched from the tower.

I don't know if there was a crazy T-shirt that Rone didn't like when he lived with us. Somewhere he found one that advertised 7 Up... sort of. On the front it said, "Make 7." Printed on the back were the words, "Up Yours!" If I only knew how it would be put to use the first time I saw it and rolled my eyes.

During the summer of the year he lived with us there was a need for someone to mow the church lawn. I knew Rone could use the money so I recommended him to the Trustees and they hired him. One Saturday I was driving by the church building on my way to the parsonage and I burst out laughing. There was Rone mowing the lawn wearing the 7 Up T Shirt. As he made his turn from the road, heading past the Penfield United Methodist Church Sign, the message on the back of his T shirt could be clearly seen by any passerby. It read, "Up Yours!" Hahaha.

Well, Rone has settled into civilian life after finishing his tour of duty. He has his own family and is using the GI Bill to finish college. He is heading towards a career in the medical field with a major in Diagnostic Sonography. I don't know if he still has that T but I know he lights up a room with his wit and wackiness!

Rone, mowing and with Bev at graduation.

"LET'R BLOW"

The Penfield United Methodist Church Board of Trustees, charged with overseeing the church building and grounds, was made up of mostly older men who had been a part of the church for many years. They did an effective job of managing the 20 acres of property. But they were very conservative when it came to spending money from the MMI Fund - Major Maintenance and Improvement fund. In fact, they had an obsession about not running this fund below $10.000. Their reasoning was, "Just in case the boiler blows."

As time went on we became fast friends with Ed and Joanne. They were both very involved in the life of the church. Ed drove to the church and back to their home - 20 miles each way - at least twice a week. In fact, when my sister, Paula, died in the late 90's, Ed and Joanne drove three hours to Jamestown, NY, to attend her Memorial Service.

In addition to attending Sunday services he helped lead the Senior High Youth Group. The young people responded enthusiastically to Ed and a woman named Donna, who provided great leadership. It was inspiring to have 10-15 high school students sitting together during the Contemporary Service.

One way to describe Ed is that he was - and is - a laid back guy. He and Donna made a wonderful team because they balanced each other. Donna kept things focused and organized while Ed provided the youth a relaxed father-figure. The kids just loved both and I will always be immensely thankful for their leadership and influence. They made a special impact for the Lord on Jed and Jeanna.

In one of my earliest conversations with Ed he told me that he had once been the president of the Board of Trustees. He noted the Trustee's obsession with keeping at least $10,000 in the MMI Fund just in case the boiler blows. In confirming their conservative ways, he expressed his ongoing opinion when he declared, "As far as I'm concerned, LET'R BLOW!"

I decided that from then on, he would be known as "Let'r Blow." It fit his personality so well and met my criteria as a humorous nickname. Just last night at a Rotary Board meeting, with Ed present, I explained to a board member how he got this nickname. To this day, when we are together - around a bonfire, in church, at Rotary, on a Cruise, or in some other context - I refer to him as Let'r Blow. Now other friends, having had me explain how he came by this moniker, and knowing his laid-back style, also call him Let'r Blow.

We are like brothers and I can hear his response when I address him as Let'r Blow! "Yesssss?"

Ed and I at my installation as Red Jacket Rotary President in June 2016

"KAMIKAZE SUSHI BAR"

Answering machines can present even a parsonage family with an opportunity to be creative. Thus, was the case at one point in Penfield. My nephew, Jack, was visiting us. He had stopped by on his way between Jamestown, NY and Long Island, where he lived. He is one of my sister's sons. Jack and his brother, Jeff, were like our sons before we had Jed. These guys used to spend a week with us in the summer when I served the Arkport congregation.

Jack has a creative - some would say twisted - sense of humor. He has always been good at mimicking people. While staying with us overnight he entertained us with a shtick he put together involving an imagined voice message at a Sushi Bar. His rendition of a man with a Japanese accent was totally convincing and hilarious. I found it so funny I invited him to create a new voice message on the parsonage phone answering machine. WHAT was I thinking??

The message went something like this: "Hero, you have reached Kamikaze Sushi Bar in downtown Tokyo. We not here right now, so reave message and we get back to you as soon as possible." I got the biggest kick out of it. But some people trying to get a hold of us didn't think it was funny.

My insurance agent from another community tried to call me and thought he had gotten the wrong number. A couple of people told me they couldn't figure out what was going on so they hung up. And one parishioner by the name of Grace let me know exactly what she thought about this bizarre greeting. Grace was like a Mom to Bev and I and like a grandma to our kids. She was in her eighties, spent time in our home for some holidays and although she had a great sense of humor, she failed to see comedy in this. She didn't mince words when she told me that she had tried to call the parsonage and got a "sushi bar" instead. "Totally Inappropriate" were her words.

Callers were once again greeted with a "You have reached the Penfield United Methodist Parsonage" message rather than thinking they had reached the "Kamikaze Sushi Bar in downtown Tokyo!"

"MACK'S WILD KINGDOM"

I am departing somewhat from my reflecting on my 33 years of pastoral ministry to share about a friend I shall call "Mack." I say "somewhat" because Mack came into the Penfield United Methodist Church family while I was the pastor but the incidents I will describe happened more recently. And what provoked this reflection was his asking me if I was going to "include him in my book." During a conversation I had with him, he suggested titling this reflection, "Trailer Park Adventures."

Mack is retired after working for years for an air rifle manufacturer. Up until recently he lived in a mobile home park on the edge of Penfield. Within this past year he moved into a home he bought in a northern suburb of Rochester. If you engage Mack in conversation, plan to be there for a while. He will talk your ear off and has a way of bringing the focus to politics, photography or guns. That sometimes truth is stranger than fiction would describe a number of things involving Mack over the years.

The first incident that happened during Mack's thirty years living in the Mobile Home Park involved a snake. He got up one morning and discovered that he had no hot water. He immediately went to the hot water tank and found that it felt cold. As he bent down to remove the shield from the pilot light he jumped back. There was a Boa Constrictor curled up underneath the hot water tank! Thinking fast he grabbed a shovel and attempted to chop its head off!! When this proved impossible, the shovel being too dull, he smashed its head in! Apparently, the slithering intruder had accessed the tank through a hatch on the outside of the trailer. Mack imagined how he could have had "company" in his bedroom! Musing where such a creature could have come from in Penfield - in a trailer park - I remembered a young couple who lived in this park who had such a snake for a "pet."

The second incident involved a Pit Bull. A man who lived in a home on an adjoining lot owned two of these dogs. They were known to be vicious, barking and lunging wildly at anyone who passed by. Occasionally one or both would break away from their chains (or somehow pry open the door) and run menacingly through the neighborhood. Many people, including Mack, had complained to the management but to no avail, until the day Mack got his gun. On that day one of the dogs escaped his chain and Mack saw him attempting to attack a neighbor, driving her inside her home. He had had enough of this menace to society and loaded his shotgun. Stepping out onto his porch he fired a couple of blasts into the ground as the dog lunged towards him.

The Pit Bull took off yelping and it was not long before the cops showed up and confiscated that gun as well as several others that he legally owned. This "Wild Kingdom" episode ended about three months later with a judge dismissing the case, Mack having his guns returned to him and the dog being euthanized. Many people had come to his defense, including the woman he was protecting.

A third adventure occurred when one-day Mack discovered a four-foot-long Iguana on his porch trying to get into his trailer through the cat door! We laughed about how he might have come home to find it curled up on his couch. Thankfully, it was a "friendly" reptile and allowed Mack to pick it up by the tail. He took it back to its owner in a garbage bag!

Not every "Wild Kingdom" incident occurred inside the trailer park, and that's a big reason why I prefer my title to the one that Mack suggested – it is more expansive.

Mark, referred to in other Penfield reflections, describes Mack as sometimes being a "screwball." (aren't we all?}

One Sunday morning, Mark was serving as worship leader. Suddenly he stopped and could hardly contain himself. Mack, seated in a front pew, suddenly jumped up, raised his leg, and slammed his foot down on a bug. The spectacle of Mack, abruptly lunging out of his seat and the sound of him slapping of his foot on the floor, startled (and amused) more than a few people. Apparently in his mind, this bug had to be stopped before further advancing into the congregation!

Finally, I must mention a comment Mack made during a conversation I was having with someone else. After a Memorial Service, a few years ago I was talking to a man named Jay and he asked me if I had used an object to eulogize a woman named Marion. I recalled that I had but before I could describe to him what it was, Mack, who had been listening in, blurted out, "WAS IT A SHRUNKEN HEAD?!"

It took me a minute or two to regain my composure before I told both Jay and Mack that it was a hand painted dish that Marion had made and given to Bev and me. And to this day, Mack, many times grinning from ear to ear, entertains and amazes me with the crazy twists and turns of his life, through the Wild Kingdom.

"BROKEN EVERY LAW OF MOVING!"

Our last move to a church was the most chaotic of all our moves. We hired a small moving company located in Canandaigua to move us from Penfield to our Canandaigua First United Methodist Church parsonage on Main Street. We were almost ready for the movers when they arrived at eight o'clock in the morning on moving day. I will return to the "almost" later in this reflection. I told them right away that they were going to need more than the two small trucks that appeared. I had several stacks of banana boxes full of books in my office, plus three file cabinets and some furniture. At the parsonage, there was an immense amount of furniture and packed goods representing a five-person family.

Sure enough, they had to send for a third truck. When they reached three trucks-full there was no room for our well used grill and Bev's old bike. These items were not going to fit into our cars, which were packed full. So, my solution to this was to leave the grill beside a shed that was used for storing church lawn equipment, semi-hidden from view. And I sent the bike flying into a tangle of brush and trees that provided a break between the parsonage and the church building. When I think of this I still laugh - Bev doesn't think it was very funny.

Now back to the "almost" in "almost ready" above, and what provokes the most laughter. Bev was in her first years of working full time for Monroe County in Child Protective Services. She could not take as much time off as she would have liked. So, we did the best job we could to prepare for the move to Canandaigua. The day before the movers arrived Suzanne and Mary came in to help Bev finish packing up the kitchen. I don't remember how many times that day I drove to Wegman's Grocery Store for more boxes. There was still considerable disarray at midnight when Mark, who I mentioned in the first Penfield reflection, showed up to pick up his wife, Suzanne, and to see how things were progressing.

I can still see the look on his face as he walked into the kitchen and exclaimed, "I can't believe this...what a mess... you've BROKEN EVERY LAW OF MOVING!!" I was dead tired and immediately burst into laughter, asking, "Why? Is there a book with laws for moving??!!" In the meantime, Mark took his arm and began scooping everything he could into a box as I continued to laugh. Thank the Lord for laughable moments during those most trying of times.

Maybe it was that fit of laughter that helped keep me awake for a couple more hours. Later that day we made the move to Canandaigua where once again, I would discover that sometimes Truth is stranger than fiction - that funny stuff just happens!

CANANDAIGUA

2004 - 2009

"BAT TONGS"

As we settled into the parsonage in Canandaigua we discovered we would be dealing with an occasional uninvited guest. My first encounter with one of these was on a warm summer Sunday evening when Jed and I were sitting in the family room watching TV. Suddenly a bat soared past us! No one had mentioned that this could happen because we lived in one of the big old homes on Main Street in Canandaigua.

This first encounter led to many other encounters over the five years we spent in this wonderful place. The Canandaigua parsonage was one of our favorites. In the first months after we moved in the Trustees had the 100-year-old wood floors refinished, new area carpets laid, the downstairs walls painted according to Bev's wishes, and all new kitchen appliances installed. Throughout the house were the old steam radiators which hissed and clanked when heated. There were five bedrooms on the second floor. It was a most welcoming and comfortable home for our family and guests.

The only challenge was dealing with those unwelcome winged creatures. I used a strobe light in the third-floor walk-in attic all night long during "bat season" to help control their intrusion. I found that it was true, they don't like flashing light. People kidded me about this light because it could be seen from Main Street through a large attic window, flashing on and off through the night. A woman in the congregation told me one Sunday morning, "I saw a bat disco taking place last night." And one midnight a policeman banged on our front door. He told us that someone driving by had reported a possible fire in our attic!

But dealing with bats in the parsonage was no laughing matter, for the most part. It was impossible to eliminate their presence, so I figured out a way to hasten their exit. I had two tennis rackets which I never used and they became my "bat rackets." One was strategically placed on each floor. I developed a tactical routine.

When one invaded our space, I would grab a bat racket, position myself in a doorway or hallway, and as the thing flew towards me I would swat it down - normally they were just knocked unconscious. Next, I would get my "bat tongs," a pair of long handled tongs I used for grilling (pictured below and on the front cover). I would slide the spatula side of the tongs under the stunned bat and firmly grasping it, I would toss it out the door. The very last step in my routine was to sanitize both the racket and tongs using Clorox.

My multi-use of those tongs though led to a very funny exchange between my friend, Ken, and I. One day I was grilling up some burgers for a staff picnic, Ken, who was the Coordinator of Adults in Ministry, took notice of the tongs I was using and asked me, "Are those the same tongs you use to pick up bats?"

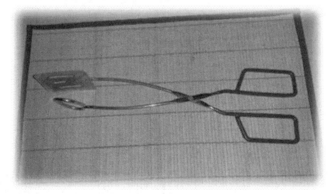

Chuckling, I said, "Yes." I roared at his follow up comment, *"I'D BETTER NOT FIND ANY BAT WINGS IN MY BURGER!"*

"FLYING AIR CONDITIONER!"

I not only had a really nice office/study in the Canandaigua First United Methodist Church building but I also had a great office staff. Judy was and still is the Office Manager and Barb was the Assistant.

Efficiency with grace and excellence would describe anything handled by these two women. They made my life as the pastor so much easier from an administrative perspective. And to top it off both had a great sense of humor.

Humor is always appreciated when it comes to dealing with daily routines, weekly responsibilities and the inevitable surprise that occurs. By surprise I mean sudden equipment failure, someone coming in or calling with a strange need or request, or an unanticipated mishap occurring in simply working together, especially with me.

One of these mishaps happened one morning that brought surprise/shock, relief and then hilarity. It was late spring and air conditioners had been put in the windows of both my study and the office complex the night before. Since the windows in this 100-year-old building were of the old larger type, the conditioners needed to be positioned just right with any open space sealed by weather stripping and extenders. This was mainly because bats need only the smallest of holes to enter. When I arrived from the parsonage next door I noticed that the weather stripping in the office complex needed further adjustment for bat proofing. This meant slightly opening the window.

I decided to climb into action. I say "climb" because I had to step up onto a counter just below the window. Kneeling, I carefully slid up the window. Knowing how easy it would be for the air conditioner to fall out, I secured it with one hand while I re-positioned the stripping. Somehow my hold on it wasn't enough and out she went! It disappeared with the power cord, which had been yanked out of the outlet, trailing behind like a kite tail. I heard it crash to the pavement two stories below and still kneeling on the counter I exclaimed (among other things), "THE AIR CONDITIONER!"

Judy and Barb came running into this outer office from their desks in the other room and shouted, "WHAT HAPPENED?!" I tried to explain this shocking turn of events. They followed with the question, "What about Ruth's car?" Ruth was our Church Treasurer who was working somewhere else in the building and she was in the habit of parking her car right below the window. Fortunately, the air conditioner had JUST missed the front end of her car when it crash-landed. Even before the replacement for the demolished unit arrived we were laughing at the thought of Pastor Jeff's "Flying Air Conditioner."

"COMMUNION STUMBLE"

Over 33 years of full time pastoral ministry there were many funny incidents connected with leading worship and preaching. I have mentioned some of these in previous reflections - the annihilation of a cluster fly doing a death spin on my Bible, a failed attempt at using Joy in a children's moment, Jed's mimic while I was preaching, and a sermon snoozer.

In Canandaigua, my last stop before retirement, I had funny stuff happen between the sound technician and me during worship. This included the microphone suddenly going dead while I was speaking and crazy hats appearing on his head, etc. At that time, the console was "hidden away" in a balcony so that the congregation would without warning see me look up and laugh. But the most hilarious incident happened during a communion service.

We served communion once a month on the first Sunday. At the front of the sanctuary there was a multilevel platform. The alter rails were located on the front edge of the first level. Then there was a step up to the level of the lectern and pulpit. Finally, at the back and on a third level sat the Communion Table. I used laypersons as stewards to help serve people as they came forward to take communion at the rails.

One Sunday during communion these stewards were serving while I stood by to replenish the juice and bread as needed. At one point, I had gone to the table on the third level and picked up a tray with cups full of grape juice in each hand. As I turned around to take these trays to the servers I forgot about the step down to the second level. I stumbled and found myself careening towards the alter rails full of kneeling people. Almost out of control, I still had to deal with the step down to the level of the rails and a picture of my taking flight into these people flashed before me.

I will never forget the looks on their faces as they saw me coming at them. They were horrified as they prepared to have me crash land with the "blood of our Lord" dumped all over them! Almost miraculously I managed to regain my balance and stagger to an upright posture just before that last step down and JUST before reaching these folks. Handing the trays to the servers I tried to assume the comportment and dignity of a robed clergy person presiding at communion. It proved impossible after coming that close to destroying any semblance of sacred order. I dissolved into the silliest of grins which I could NOT wipe off my face for the rest of the service. That grin returns every time I think about this.

"I'M GOING TO PUT IT DOWN!"

One afternoon I was returning from a physical therapy session. I was recovering from having my right knee scoped due to a meniscus tear. As I drove up the driveway between the Canandaigua parsonage and an apartment building next door I noticed some commotion near an Ontario County Animal Control truck parked in a small lot. After parking behind our garage, I walked over to see what was happening.

Several family members who lived in one of the apartments were watching an Animal Control Officer walking under and around a second story porch. The porch was surrounded with lattice work, including a door that allowed entrance. Several 32-gallon garbage cans were kept there, out of sight. Quite a ruckus was occurring as this officer, holding a long pole with a loop on one end, had opened the door and was in the process of tossing around those garbage cans. The young father of the family told me that a raccoon had wandered through the back yard and disappeared under the porch. The officer was struggling to corner the coon so that he could drop the loop over its head and remove it from the property. The animal was almost trapped. But this young man and I noticed that there was still a possible escape route between the steps down from the porch and the corner of the house. So, we decided to be helpful and try to block this route. He picked up a large rock, holding it above his head. As we stood in this gap suddenly the raccoon poked out its head. My neighbor threw down the rock, preventing an escape. I categorize what happened next as bizarre.

In no time, the Animal Control Officer was in our faces reaming us out because we had thrown a rock at this raccoon! His rant went something like this, "WHAT'S THE MATTER WITH YOU? IS THIS THE WAY YOU TREAT AN ANIMAL? YOU THROW ROCKS AT IT???!!" We stood there in total disbelief. Here we thought we were helping this man by keeping the coon under the porch so he could catch it and he was reprimanding us! Well, the next series of events sealed the "truth is stranger than fiction" nature of this experience.

We watched the officer finally drop the loop over the cornered coon and then drag it out from under the porch. I thought he was going to put it into a cage I saw in the back of his truck. Instead he hoisted the flailing animal and dropped it into one of the garbage cans he had also pulled out from under the porch. As he peered into the garbage can he said these barely audible words, "I'm going to put it down!" With a small crowd that included some children watching, he went to his truck and pulled out a rifle. Pointing it into the garbage can he fired off some shots - "BLAM! BLAM! BLAM!" The young father and I were incredulous as we looked at each other thinking, "What Just Happened?!" After all, he had just yelled at us for "throwing a rock... at this (poor) animal!"

Well, the life of a possible rabid raccoon ended in a blaze of gunfire, a 32-gallon garbage can was ventilated, a stunned crowd walked away in complete disbelief, and I had another crazy event in the life of a pastor to ponder.

"COP STOP"

I had few run-ins with the law during my 33 years of full time service as a pastor. The first time I remember being stopped for speeding was when I failed to observe a speed limit change coming into the village of Arkport. It was dark and I sped by a 35 mile an hour sign doing 55. Fortunately, the town cop knew me from playing basketball at the high school on Thursday nights and said, upon seeing me in his flashlight beam, "Oh, it's you (the pastor)!" He let me off with an encouraging word or two.

Then there was another time, also during my eleven years in Arkport, when I must have gotten a ticket. I remember someone providing me with THEIR copy of a "police blotter" column from our local paper with something cute, like, "Look what Kilroy found." Parishioners found this more laughable than I did.

The last time I was held accountable for breaking the law was when I was a pastor in Canandaigua. I think it was amazing that according to my recollection it was twenty years between cop stops! At the time, this occurred I saw nothing particularly funny about it. In fact, I was pretty bummed, but, as in many other experiences in life, humor can be seen afterwards.

One afternoon I was heading out to the Ontario County Health Facility to check on some parishioners. I was on Ontario Street, still within the Canandaigua city limits, and came up behind a guy driving a backhoe. The speed limit was 30 but he was traveling no faster than 10 miles an hour. I grew very frustrated, wondering how long I was going to have to follow him. There was a double solid line down the middle of the street but I could see way off in the distance and there was no car coming from the other direction. So, I gunned it and drove around the backhoe. No sooner had I re-crossed the double solid line to get back into my lane than I saw red lights flashing behind me.

I pulled over hoping the police car was going for someone else - there was no one else. It wasn't long before I had a young Canandaigua Police officer at my window, asking me for my license, registration and insurance card. She asked me if I knew why she had pulled me over and I said, "Yes." But I didn't stop with that. I continued admitting that I HAD crossed double solids to pass the backhoe. I justified it by saying, "There were NO cars coming in the opposite direction." And I pleaded, "Why should I have to drive 10 miles an hour for who knows how long?"

She didn't buy it. I was really annoyed with that and the fact that she kept addressing me as, "Mr. Crawford." (I didn't give much thought as to how else she was supposed to address me) When she returned from her car she handed me a ticket and as nicely as possible, calling me, "Mr. Crawford," told me to appear at such and such a date and time to answer for my law breaking. Well, I hoped that all of this was going to remain hidden from church and community folks but it was not to be. Somehow it got around and before I knew it there was a toy backhoe sitting on my study desk! My comedic parishioners didn't want me to forget this trespass - this cop stop - ever!

"CEMETARY UNZIPPED"

There was a precious woman named Barb in the Canandaigua congregation. She had been a part of the life of the church and the community for many years. In years past she had served on the staff as a part time pastoral assistant helping with the ministry of visitation. When I arrived, Barb was in her early 80's. She let me know right away that she wanted to be helpful in any way she could. She would occasionally stop by my study just to check on me and see how things were going.

Barb and I became good friends and I counted on her help with Memorial and Funeral services. She was loved and highly respected by the church family and knew many people in the community through her involvement with Rotary and Kiwanis and a visitation ministry in the local hospital. She had a gift for working with families who had experienced a death and loved developing detailed eulogies. Many times, and especially when I didn't know the person who had died nearly as long as she had, I would turn to her to talk about the life of the deceased.

On one occasion Barb and I were asked to do a grave-side service. It became the funniest experience I had in all my years of performing this kind of ministry. The service was set for 1pm in the Woodlawn Cemetery in Canandaigua. I had gone to the Y for a workout during the lunch hour and rushed home to shower and put on my suit. I arrived at the cemetery at the appointed hour and with Barb at my side I began with words of comfort and some Scripture readings. At some point, I felt a slight breeze in my midsection and had the horrible thought that I hadn't zipped my fly. As unobtrusively as I could I slid my right index finger down to that area and sure enough, as they say, the "barn door" was open.

Barb and I were standing in front of something like 25 people and my suit coat was NOT buttoned so I really had to concentrate on my reading while slightly turning away from the mourners. As I finished all I could think of was how I was going to zip up. Thankfully it was Barb's turn to pray! So, while she invoked the Lord's comfort I sought relief from my embarrassment behind the crowd. Hoping that all eyes were closed I began a slow backpedal seeking to get behind everyone so that I could... Git'r Done.

Barb was finishing and I was almost at the back. I was parallel with two attractive and well-dressed young women when I stopped and zipped. As I looked out of the corner of my eyes I saw the unthinkable. They were looking directly at me and had probably watched me take every slow step backwards, wondering what in the world I was doing. Well, they found out when they saw me, the pastor, reach for my fly. And I imagine that they even heard the zipping sound in the tranquility of that place of the departed. Red faced, I had to try to act normal as I returned to the front.

Barb burst out laughing when I shared it with her later. And those two women must have had quite a wacky story to tell about the pastor who was unzipped in the cemetery!

"TERMINATOR AND JESUS"

A year or so before I retired someone showed me a video clip produced by Mad TV. It involved a ridiculous but hilarious parody weaving Jesus' mission to die for our sins with the sudden appearance of the Terminator. From that moment, I knew that in the wacky world of Pastor Jeff this "would preach" as they say. I will attempt to unpack the nutty story line of "Terminator Three - The Greatest Action Story Ever Told."

It is December 25, 0000. Bolts of lightning and electric power arcs fly around as the Terminator, an Arnold Schwarzenegger impersonator, emerges naked, out of a bubble, on a street in Bethlehem. The Terminator's first order of business is to find clothes. So, with his retinal scan camera vision he spots the three Wise Men coming along the street with their camels. Their friendly greeting is met with a demand for their clothes. At this, one of the Wise Men tells him that they come bearing fine gifts but their clothes aren't one of them. The Terminator then asks him if he is "some-kind of wise guy." To which he says, "Why, yes." It earns him a punch that provides "Arnold" with something to cover his naked body. With this he leaves Bethlehem.

He next appears as Jesus is teaching and feeding thousands near Nazareth. Roman soldiers are coming to take Jesus into custody when the Terminator shows up with a shot gun. He takes out the soldiers to Jesus' consternation and then says to Jesus, "Come with me if you want to live." Jesus asks him, "What are you doing?!" To which the Terminator responds, "trying to protect you." Jesus tries to tell the Terminator that it is supposed to be like this and that he can't "go around killing people!" Jesus then prays for forgiveness for this "robot from the future."

Next, Jesus is gathered with his disciples in the Upper Room for the last supper. As Jesus tells them to eat, the door bursts open and the Terminator exclaims, "eat this," as he sends Judas flying across the communion table with a shotgun blast. He shoots Judas three times, declaring his determination to protect Jesus from the betrayer sent to terminate him!

An increasingly agitated Jesus keeps raising him from the dead, and shouts, "You just don't get it, do you? I am SUPPOSED to die for the sins of mankind!"

The last scene involves Jesus coming through Jerusalem with the cross. A woman in the crowd is weeping at the spectacle. But the Terminator, standing next to her with his shotgun on his shoulder, puts his arm around her and says, "Don't worry, He'll be back."

Well, I really wanted to find a way to use this clip in a sermon. But you can imagine it was not an easy illustration to use, since it bordered on inappropriate. I finally found a way. It was during my last Lenten season before retirement. I was preparing a sermon with a focus on Jesus' strength through weakness as he journeyed to the Cross. THAT was the perfect context to fit in "Terminator and Jesus!" The Terminator only knew violence and destruction to accomplish his purpose - like the world too often does. What a contrast to Jesus!!

I am not sure how well it went over. I didn't dare to ask. My Canandaigua congregation had grown quite used to my wackiness by then. But one of my staff, who

I believe showed me this clip in the first place, came up to me afterwards and exclaimed, "I CAN'T BELIEVE YOU USED 'TERMINATOR AND JESUS!'" I burst out laughing and said, "Why? I thought it fit really well and after all, what did I have to lose (I was only three months from retirement)?!" To this day, he still says the same thing, "I CAN'T BELIEVE THAT YOU USED...." HAHAHAHA.

"CELEBRATION!"

The day arrived for my retirement celebration. My Canandaigua First United Methodist Church family put together quite an event. Julie and Paul led the service of celebration, which was full of photos, testimonies, laughter and music. It covered more than just my five years in Canandaigua. Thirty- three years of pastoral ministry were summed up and God was praised for His faithfulness and grace. A dinner followed in the fellowship hall and other rooms decorated with Penn State and Kentucky Wildcat colors. Over 300 were in attendance and we were presented with a $4,000 check!

One of the many highlights involved the presence  of my best friend from seminary. Tom was my roommate then and we shared many emotional and, shall we say inventive (wacky) moments that stretched out over the years of pastoral ministry. I took part in his wedding as our seminary days came to an end. And our friendship has deepened since. We have spent many hours talking pastoral ministry and theology on the phone and Bev and I have been in Tom and Pam's home several times. He is the pastor of two United Methodist Churches on the edge of Lynchburg, Virginia.

After graduation from Asbury Theological Seminary, Tom served as a pastor in California and then moved to England where he earned a PhD in Theology. In more recent years he has served on the faculty of Asbury and is in his second pastoral appointment in the Virginia Conference.

An example of Tom's inventiveness is a list he developed during the time we lived in the single men's dorm on the seminary campus in Wilmore, Kentucky. He used his initials, which are H.O.T - Howe Octavious Thomas - in calling this list, "HOT'S Sure Shots." Like every other single guy, I was on the bottom of the list until I met Bev, who was a student on the Asbury

College campus. As our relationship got more serious I moved up the list and I finally reached the top - became a Sure Shot - when we were engaged. That list still existed years after we graduated and students wondered WHO had started it. Well, it was HOT!

There are many funny stories I could tell about Tom and me, like the costumes we used to make for Halloween, etc. But to have this good friend of mine come up from Virginia so that he could participate in my Retirement Celebration was amazing. We had a great time for a couple of days before the party and he was his very serious and sometimes very screwball self. We toured Fairport one afternoon and as

Tom stood along the Erie Canal watching the boat traffic and then the Lift Bridge go up he did one of his crazy impressions.

He suddenly became a modern-day John Wesley (the eighteen-century founder of Methodism), raising both arms and pronouncing a blessing on everyone riding on the Colonial Bell Canal Boat! I burst out laughing as I felt deeply the privilege of fulfilling the call of the Lord on my life to serve as a pastor.

Post Retirement
Reflections

2009 - Present

"SQUEEKY"

I am putting the finishing touches on these reflections. Since retirement, people have asked me if someone can really be retired from pastoral work. I tell them something like this: "Yes, I am really retired but I still do pastoral things when asked, like fill in as emergency pastor for a limited period of time, or preach or officiate at "weddings."

A startling and hilarious event occurred one Sunday morning several years ago while filling the pulpit for a friend. It happened in a small church on the north side of Rochester. As I sat down beside the pulpit, ready for the service to begin, I noticed that a sparse crowd had gathered. The small pew I occupied was sideways to the congregation so I could both observe it, and the persons joining me on the platform who would be participating in the service.

I was struck by the choir as it filed in to assume its place. It was made up of mostly older men and women with at least one notable exception. Right in the middle of this group was a younger man who I estimated to be at least 6' 5". The really odd thing was the way they seated themselves. Rather than sitting in rows they sat in one long line that extended across the back of the platform. I smiled at the thought there were as many people on the platform as in the sanctuary!

The service began with some announcements by the worship leader and then the choir stood for a choral call to worship. I was not looking at them until I heard what I thought was a strange prolonged squeaky noise. My immediate thought was that someone had passed gas. But then, on second thought, I said to myself, "Not in church?!" It came from the direction of the choir and so I slowly turned my head in that direction. Rolling eyes and contorted looks would best describe what I saw. A couple of the members were looking at the tall drink of water, whose face was beet red. It left no doubt as to the identity of "Squeaky!"

In all of my 33 years of full time pastoral ministry and then in this fill-in role since retirement, I had never experienced anything quite like this... this... flatulence in church.

Bev was sitting in a pew all by herself and when I asked her if she had heard what had happened all I can say is that her response was priceless!!

BROTHER GREG

This is a second Reflection that falls into a category involving pastoral ministry following retirement. "Squeaky" was the first. While my friendship with Greg was of a more serious nature during the time I served as pastor in Canandaigua, he knew how to tickle my funny bone. I discovered just how intent Greg was in being a disciple of Jesus when we had some focused conversations and he joined a Lenten Small Group Study in our home. He was one of those people in the congregations I served who refreshed my own faith and focus.

I loved Greg's sense of humor, most of the time. He had this way of interjecting a quip or one liner that took off from something that was said and then giggling as his face scrunched up. It was infectious and lit up a room. I enjoyed his humor even more after I retired and took up golf. Greg and I became golfing buddies, often riding in a cart together. I regularly advised him to "get a new 'Joke Book'." He loved golf even though at times it didn't love him back. He was infamous among the Canandaigua First UMC Friday Golf Crew for hitting the ball really hard somewhere – into the water, the woods or...into next week when it went straight! Every course we played kept some of Greg's Titlists. One time he demolished his driver by laying into a shot off the T to the extent that he paused at the Club House to buy a new one!

The beautiful thing is that Greg enjoyed the game no matter what and we always found something about which to laugh. We agreed many times that "Fairway golf is overrated" and "Military Golf (left, right, left) can be interesting." He maintained his sense of humor even after being diagnosed with cancer and battling it until he went to be with the Lord at age 47.

Greg's four priorities were Jesus first, family second (Brenda, Brittany and Virgil), Church third and then... golf. I was privileged to be involved in the marriage of Greg to Brenda, the love of his life. And I delighted in seeing Greg's son, Virgil, come home to the family, joining Brittany. I assisted in Greg's Memorial Service and used a gift certificate from Brenda to buy what I call my "Greg Seaborn Memorial Golf Ball Retriever." I have used it many times and am reminded of my unique and lovable brother in Christ with quite a funny bone. As I look up I say, "Love you Greg!"

Here I am demonstrating the use of the "Greg Seaborn Memorial Golf Ball Retriever" during Children's Moments at Canandaigua First UMC. I was filling in for the pastor and my focus was on how Jesus retrieved Greg and how he retrieves us!

Biographical Information

Born: August 8, 1945 in Jamestown, New York

Raised in Kansas and New York

Graduated from Frewsburg Central in Chautauqua County, New York – 1963

Served in the US Army as a Motion Picture Photographer from November 1964 – November 1967

Attended Jamestown Community College in 1968-69

Graduated from Houghton College in 1972 with a B.A. in Religion

Graduated from Asbury Theological Seminary in 1976 with a Master of Divinity Degree

Met my wife, Beverly, while a seminary student and we married in December 1975

We have three beautiful children, daughter in law, soon to be son in law and three grandchildren

Retired for eight years after serving for 33 years in full time pastoral ministry – this included five appointments

Live in Fairport, New York

Proverbs 17:22 A joyful heart is good medicine, but a crushed spirit dries up the bones.

Humor is medicine to the soul.

God so DEFINITELY has a sense of humor!!

Made in the USA
Lexington, KY
05 November 2019